Gentlemen Only

Gentlemen Only

AN INSIDER'S LOOK AT GOLF
IN AUGUSTA, GEORGIA,
AND WHAT SHE FOUND AT THE
END OF MAGNOLIA LANE

ROBBIE WILLIAMS AND LEE HEFFERNAN

TowleHouse Publishing
Nashville, Tennessee

TowleHouse books are distributed by National Book Network
(NBN), 4720 Boston Way, Lanham, Maryland 20706.

Library of Congress Cataloging-in-Publication data is available.
ISBN: 1-931249-12-1

Some of the people referred to in this book have been given
fictitious names to protect their privacy.

Cover design by Gore Studio, Inc.
Page design by Mike Towle

Printed in the United States of America
2 3 4 5 6 — 06 05 04 03 02

To Sara, the schoolteacher in our family, who teaches young children to read and love books

CONTENTS

PROLOGUE

On my second or third trip down Magnolia Lane and onto the grounds of Augusta National Golf Club, I entered the front foyer of the main clubhouse instead of going directly to the pro shop. The entrance hall was typical of many older homes in the Augusta area. It was small and in no way ostentatious as an outsider might imagine, but rather it was functional in nature and understated in decor. On the wall to my left was an apparatus that resembled some kind of small scoreboard on which a few names of members were listed. I later learned that this was how the front-desk employees knew which members were on the property, from the time they entered the gate on Washington Road until they left the premises. To say the least, I was impressed with this attention to detail, but the thing that really caught my eye and held my attention for a while was a highly polished brass plaque mounted on the staircase to my right. Even though small in size, there was something about this plaque that said more than just which gender was allowed up the stairs. *Gentlemen Only* was a term Clifford Roberts used as his standard for membership at the Augusta National. The implication and the truth was that this place had a great deal to do with establishing and maintaining proper conduct, strict discipline, and, most of all, total control.

PREFACE

Clifford Roberts was able to do something that no other person has been able to do. He created a Garden of Eden in which to preserve the legend of Bobby Jones. He was able to not only create this place, Augusta National Golf Club, but he was able to enhance the legend and give it a permanent resting place with all the elegance and style that Bobby Jones personified. A resting place is not unusual, but a resting place that provides an environment allowing growth is unique. Anyone who has ever been to the Augusta National will attest to the fact that this is an adequate description of this place created to house and protect the legend and legacy of the great Bobby Jones.

Mr. Roberts could best be described as a disciplinarian—a disciplinarian in its purest form. Those who have used the words despot, dictator, and other such inappropriate terms to characterize him did not truly understand one very important thing about the man. The same rules that he so strictly enforced on others he applied to himself in an even more rigid manner. This was a place he created and guarded ferociously, but when he was on the property, he abided by the rules like the rest of the membership. If Mr. Roberts had a piece of toasted pound cake or a sliced chicken sandwich, which he did frequently, he always was billed for the food. The strict rule about no fivesomes on the course applied to him just as it did to all the other men.

A funny story about just such an incident occurred one lazy Sunday afternoon when only five members showed up to play the course. Since games were always arranged by the golf pro, it was Bob Kletcke's delicate duty to go to the Trophy Room, a part of the clubhouse used for dining and other functions, to explain that it would be necessary for them to divide up and play as a threesome and a twosome. This arrangement did not please the gentlemen at all. They started arguing with Bob, hoping they could persuade him to let them play as a fivesome. He would not even consider their pleadings. His answer was backed up with the explanation that if he allowed them to play in a fivesome, Mr. Roberts would probably be flying over in a plane and a new golf pro would take his job. The men filed out to the course as they were told and played their golf as instructed, even though they were the only people on the entire eighteen-hole course.

This kind of precise discipline often gives rise to a form of humor that those closely associated with the situation find quite funny. The austere surroundings of the Augusta National provided an incubator in which this humor grew and ripened. As the wife of a member—a wife who often played golf there—I was a witness to many such amusing scenarios. As my husband aged and was unable to play golf very often, I became the fourth for guests he was entertaining. On first hearing this, almost everyone's reaction would be "Lucky you." Sometimes that was true and sometimes it was not. After all, how many times can one point out the Eisenhower Tree at seventeen with enthusiasm and real passion? However, if guests happened to be people who could hardly contain themselves the moment they came through the front gate, well, that made it all worthwhile. Most of these truly appreciative types realized they probably would never get this opportunity again. The biggest thrill for me was to invite a local Augustan, someone who grew up in the shadow of the course and had never been there, even to see the Masters, to come out and play golf at the club. Those were among the times I most cherished at Augusta National.

In this book I share some of the stories I was privileged to witness firsthand, as well as some other stories that might be considered hearsay but which, literally true or not, help paint the big picture of golf in Augusta. For almost thirty years I quietly made notes about happenings, "mis-happenings," incidents, and "coincidents." To have been an innocent bystander in this setting is more than the average person can ever imagine, in terms of "the ridiculous and the sublime." There is a theory in golf that goes something like this: The properly struck golf ball merely gets in the way of a golf club swung properly. This might well describe what happened with golf, Augusta, Augusta National, and me. None of this was planned or manufactured. All of these things just "got in the way" as I was moving along with my little life. There's no way I could have orchestrated all this even had I tried. Instead, Augusta golf and Augusta National "happened" to me.

A few thousand stories and articles begin with the phrase, "The first time I drove down Magnolia Lane . . ." These writers then begin to relate their inner emotions with terms like "goosebumps the size of apples," "butterflies with the wings of eagles," and "nerve endings ringing like the bells in the Tower of London." However you describe it, the first trip down Magnolia Lane and onto the grounds of Augusta National is an adrenaline rush for any golfer with a genuine interest in and knowledge of the sport and its traditions. For many, that adrenaline rush is not just a one-time thing, either: Being at Augusta National never gets old. Me—I was an exception to the rule. I was an unwitting visitor to Augusta National, unaware of the club's prestige and worldwide intrigue, on the occasion of my first trip there, an excursion which had absolutely nothing to do with golf. But I'll explain that later.

I consider myself extremely lucky that it was only when I looked back that I realized where I had been and the importance and the uniqueness of the journey. Therefore I decided to put in writing how I came to know the inner sanctum of golf's "most sacred cathedral" and most of its religious lore. One of my three daughters, Lee, joined me in this venture of recalling the intertwinement of our lives and golf at Augusta, and her stories will appear periodically in this book.

My past association with this place and some people there have provided me with a repertoire of factual stories and some embellished with just enough truth to make them believable. It will not be important for the reader to discern into which category each of these accounts falls. However, it will be extremely important to keep in mind the fact that you are reading about a place like no other in the world.

—*Robbie Williams*

Lee Heffernan:

In true, understated Augusta National form, each year a small, nondescript paper directory was sent out listing each member by state and country. If you saw this directory, you would never assume it contained a roster of some of the wealthiest, most powerful people in the country. It was printed in black and white, cropped poorly, and housed in a white paper cover featuring the logo and the year. It was always interesting to peruse the amazing list of names and places of residence.

1 Gentleman Doctor

OR, "BLOODY BEGINNINGS"

Nothing that happened to me before the late 1950s prepared me for what was to come later. I grew up in a small south Georgia town, went away to a small Baptist college in middle Georgia, completed training as a medical technologist at a large municipal hospital in Georgia's largest city, Atlanta, and ended up in Augusta, Georgia, with a job working for a pathologist in a private laboratory.

This pathologist was an avid golfer with, as I would later learn, just the proper temperament needed to play the game of golf well. He was calm and extremely even-tempered in all circumstances, and he always seemed to be wearing a pleasant smile. At that time I knew nothing about the game of golf. Absolutely nothing. I had grown up with the belief that any girl who participated in any kind of athletic endeavor must be some sort of masculine freak. Most of my time in high school was spent learning and practicing the art of baton twirling and marching with the band at football games and parades. I even competed in state-level events and went to the University of Georgia summer camps to become even more adept at the art of baton twirling. I dare say I had terrific hand-eye coordination, and even though I didn't know it at the time but would find out later, I had some sort of innate skills that would translate well to swinging a golf club and guiding a little white ball around the golf course. All the while, though, as a teenager more interested in boys than birdies, I kept a suspicious eye on those girls who played sports such as basketball and tennis. That kind of activity for girls somehow just didn't seem right to me, which helps explain how I was able to reach adulthood without having ever heard of the Women's Titleholders Tournament, the Augusta National, the Masters Golf Tournament, or anything remotely connected to the game. Bobby Jones was not a household name where I came from, and golf was a game played by people with whom I had little or no contact.

A few months after I began working for this most pleasant doctor, he called from the hospital one day in April in somewhat of a snit. I barely recognized his voice. He was speaking in quick phrases, breathless with excitement. His usual calm demeanor was gone, replaced by an anxiety quite unusual for him. Hurriedly, he explained that he would be picking me up on his way to make a house call. A house call??? Making a house call is not the way laboratory medicine is practiced in the real world. At least, we had never made a house call in all the time I had been working with him. Furthermore, I had never seen this man excited or anxious about anything. He asked me to put together a lab tray using the best needles and other supplies we might need to do a venipuncture, which is the basic procedure commonly used for drawing blood from a vein. His instructions to meet him in front of the building with supplies in hand seemed more than a little odd to me. My mind was racing as I tried to get a grasp of what this was all about as I collected the needed equipment and rushed out the door. Talk about adrenaline rushes.

When we were in his car and on our way to this mystery location, he quickly explained that we were going to the Augusta National—which meant absolutely nothing to me and therefore did nothing to answer the questions bouncing around inside my head. I had never heard of Augusta National or the big golf tournament, something called the Masters, taking place at that moment. En route, the only part of our conversation that I still remember was his stated hope that some guy named Gary Player would win this particular tournament. Even with the tone of the conversation gearing down from panic to casualness, I observed that he still seemed more excited than I had ever seen him. Something big was going down, at least from his point of view.

When we turned onto Washington Road near Augusta National, I became profoundly aware that we were entering a world with which I was totally unfamiliar. Long lines of traffic, policemen everywhere, and hordes of people walking out of many different parking lots and toward our destination were clues that I was no longer in Kansas. Turning off of Washington Road and driving down Magnolia Lane amidst all the confusion of taxis, media people, and celebrities further confirmed my original assessment. I was entering a new world. We were given priority treatment, waved through the dense traffic, and directed to what I later learned is the Bobby Jones Cottage (cottage being somewhat of a modest description), located opposite Augusta National's No. 10 tee. At this point, I still did not know whom we were seeing, but I figured that he must be a very important person with lots of power.

Gentleman Doc parked his car in an appointed place, jumped out, and proceeded with haste across the lush green grass to the impeccably manicured and maintained house that held our patient. As we approached the cottage, my employer said something like, "I know you are extremely good at drawing blood, but this time it will mean a great deal to me if things go well." *What was going on???*

When the door opened, I found myself looking directly into the eyes of an older man seated beside a small table. To describe these eyes as piercing would be an understatement. These eyes demanded information

Since I wasn't aware of this man's importance or this place's world-renowned prestige, I had no reason to be nervous and was able to perform the job quickly and proficiently.

immediately. The doctor introduced himself and then presented me as the person who would be drawing the blood. As I was preparing to stick the vein, my employer explained in his kindest, most courteous voice that the small vial of blood would be used to determine the cause of the man's malaise. Since I wasn't aware of this man's importance or this place's world-renowned prestige, I had no reason to be nervous and was able to perform the job quickly and proficiently. When I had finished sticking Mr. Clifford Roberts's vein, he said, "Young lady, you are as good as those people at the Mayo Clinic, where I normally go for treatment!" I was complimented, but my boss was relieved beyond belief. Little did I know that his dream of a green jacket had just inched closer to the realm of possibility.

After we left the cottage, I had a few minutes to look around and observe what was going on around the clubhouse and out on the golf course. Observing the size of the crowd and hearing the commotion being created by great golfers unknown to me, I knew that it would be necessary someday to revisit this occurrence and educate myself about this situation. I wanted to know more. I needed to know more. Something involving this much grandeur, style, and excitement must be worth knowing all about, down to the smallest detail. My starched, white uniform and polished clinic shoes seemed more than a little out of place amidst all the bright golf attire. My entire life seemed out of place there.

When I returned to the lab, the attending physician—in fact, what seemed like all of the other doctors in town—kept calling to get the results of the blood tests. I was told to put all other work aside and to complete the diagnostic profile on Mr. Roberts as soon as possible. Of course, I did just that because even I was beginning to get caught up in the whirlwind. Upon completion of the tests, everyone concerned seemed quite relieved when it was apparent that Mr. Roberts had no major medical problem. Apparently, he had just been suffering from some minor virus or other kind of temporary ailment.

The happy ending doesn't stop there. Sometime later the Gentleman Doctor did get his green jacket, emblematic of membership at the exclusive Augusta National. I like to think that my successful venipuncture of Mr. Roberts had had a great deal to do with that. Who knows what would have happened to this doctor's dream of being a member of the Augusta National if I had missed Mr. Roberts's vein on that fine day in April when I had my first look at these hallowed grounds? Of all the Augusta

National members I would ever meet, the Gentleman Doctor deserved the honor of membership in that special fraternity more than most. His expertise at the game of golf and his gentlemanly manner exemplified the perfect profile of what an Augusta National member should be.

Over time I came to better appreciate my employer's anxiety and apprehension on that day we journeyed to the Jones Cottage to take some of Mr. Roberts's blood. This man, Mr. Roberts, had achieved a status few men can reach in a lifetime. In the coming years I would learn all about this man, as well as the club and tournament he and golfing legend Bobby Jones had founded. It occurred to me that Mr. Roberts had been getting "blood" from almost everyone he met during his life. Given this situation, I had been fortunate to turn the tables and draw a little blood from him on our first meeting.

Mr. Roberts and I would meet again. My next trip down Magnolia Lane was as the wife of a member.

2 *Gentleman Husband*

OR, "HERE
THEY ARE,
BUT YOU'LL
NEVER BE
ABLE TO HIT
'EM."

Several years went by before I would meet Clifford Roberts again. During this time, I continued to work in the small private laboratory for the Gentleman Doctor, who was enjoying his new membership at the Augusta National Golf Club. Because of his club membership, I was privy to bits and pieces of information about the National. Hardly any of this registered with me since I still knew little about Augusta or golf. But I was a quick learner and I came to find out that the city of Augusta had a rich and interesting history. The convergence here of winter tourists, various ethnic groups, and native Augustans gave the town an unusual aura. The combination of these factions, which ultimately shaped the town's history, made Augusta the ideal place to build the Augusta National and create the Masters Tournament.

In my spare time and my days off, I began to explore Augusta's history, which is so unlike that of the town in South Georgia, Fitzgerald, where I had grown up and lived most of my formative years. In my hometown that was "new" by Augusta's standards, there were no French, Irish, Italians, Greeks, Germans, Chinese, or other groups of non-English descent. Because I had not traveled extensively, I grew up believing that all cities and towns were comprised of white populations descended from a pure English background. Local residents in my hometown liked to claim their Irish ancestry on Saint Patrick's Day, but it was a claim that would vanish a day after the celebration. I had never met a pure, 100 percent Irish person until after I had moved to Augusta. Diversity did not exist where I grew up, and there were no outside influences to introduce new and different ideas. Augusta offered quite a contrast, brandishing an atmosphere ripe with all these different ethnic groups, as well as the wealthy winter tourists from the North and other parts of the country. It had been a crossroads and trading center even back to the time of DeSoto, when he came through looking for gold and treasures. George Washington and Marquis de Lafayette later paid visits.

Wealthy northern tourists were wintering in Augusta by the early 1900s, long before Florida had become the wintertime attraction it is today. The Forest Hills Hotel, the Bon Air, and the Partridge Inn were among Augusta's main attractions welcoming these strangers to their city. Activities such as hunting, golf, and various social functions were a part of life for tourists and local Augustans alike. Entertaining the northern outsiders was a natural endeavor for the locals. It's no wonder that Bobby Jones and Cliff Roberts ended their search for a site to build an exclusive golf club and course in Augusta, with its status as an established resort. The climate was ideal for conducting outdoor activities, the Fruitland Nurseries property was available, and, most of all, Augusta was comfortable hosting wealthy visitors. Also, because of the relatively small size of the city, the Augusta National would stand out as a more significant presence here than it would have in a larger city. The town was so eager to promote this venture that even average local residents bought a share or two to help this potential civic investment.

As I continued working in this laboratory as a twentysomething ingenue, some of the town's tales were laid out for me by the patients I saw regularly. The clientele who came to this private lab were a cut above the Augusta norm. To say that I came in contact with many of the "silk stocking" crowd would be an understatement. This was a new experience for me, having come from a small South Georgia town and having trained at Grady Hospital in Atlanta, a municipal hospital treating mostly patients with abnormal hemoglobin readings, which often indicate a history of poor diet and poor health. I became chummy with some of these people because I was the only employee there, and they had to return many times for repeat procedures.

Gentleman Husband

After I had been at the lab for almost a year, I met this one particular patient who came in for some hematology work. He was an older gentleman, extremely courteous but quite talkative. Later I would understand that this loquaciousness was a result of his profession: He was an attorney. When the first round of tests was completed, we discovered some of the findings were out of the normal range. It would be necessary for him to come back on a regular basis for follow-up work. On one of these subsequent visits, he asked me out to dinner with him and some of his friends. I politely refused—for many reasons. I was busy dating medical students at the time, and then there was the age discrepancy—more than thirty years. Being the proud gentleman he was, he never asked me out again—at least for a couple of years, even though he continued to be a regular patient at the laboratory.

On one of these subsequent visits, he asked me out to dinner with him and some of his friends. I politely refused—for many reasons.

After a while, something happened that changed our relationship, the results of which would alter my life significantly. One day I was driving from Augusta to Fitzgerald, Georgia, when I was involved in a minor accident with a small-town policeman, who insisted that the

"The Young Chick" and her "Old Crow."

mishap had been my fault. This simply wasn't the case, and I did not wish for my insurance company to think this policeman's facts about the accident were accurate. But it was my word against his, and obviously as a private citizen I was at a disadvantage. At this point, I figured I had no other choice but to pay my "lawyer-patient" a visit. Perhaps he would be able to write a letter on my behalf stating that I had been unjustly accused by this small-town cop. Naturally, he was overjoyed to oblige. When I arrived at his office later that afternoon after work, he was waiting there for me. Not only was he waiting past his usual office time, but he also had a warm and charming way of handling my stressful situation surrounding the accident. Later, after we were well into our relationship, he would look back and tell people about my first visit to his office. He would always say that he was there waiting patiently for a good reason—a reason summed up in the old story about the fly and the spider—"Do come in," said the spider to the fly. As for the mishap involving the belligerent policeman, my problem was taken care of very nicely and my insurance company was happy about the outcome.

As time went by, I lost interest in the medical students and became more interested in meeting people outside the medical field. When my "lawyer-patient" called to invite me to the Augusta Country Club for the Saturday night dance during Masters week, I felt a certain obligation to return the favor. I accepted the invitation, went to the dance, and had a great time. This man was a great storyteller, had a great sense of humor, and possessed impeccable manners. I had no trouble accepting his forthcoming invitations to dinner, etc.

Things moved at a rather fast pace after that. His friends were quick to tell me that he was extremely hard to please as far as women are concerned. His longtime status as Augusta's Most Eligible Bachelor was known by almost everyone in the town. More than one person had tried desperately to set him up with just the kind of woman they thought he would like. Our unusual personalities and similarly quick wits seemed to make up for all of the other differences we had as far as age, background, religion, etc., were concerned. Therefore, his close friends were excited about this new person in their old buddy's life. It became apparent to me rather quickly that these friends were like no other people with whom I had come in contact. Even their nicknames suggested a sense of intrigue—monikers such as "the Fox" and "the Bull" had me thinking there must be some mysterious inner club to which they all belonged. "The Crow" was the name assigned to my guy— a name taken from the image on the label of an Old Crow whiskey bottle. His friends told me he was so named because he had been seen more often than not decked out in a tuxedo, performing the master-of-ceremonies bit for all sorts of important social functions. This close-knit group of men played golf and cards and spent long hours telling jokes and devising plans for practical jokes. Most of this activity took place at the Augusta Country Club or on short out-of-town golf trips. A club within a club was an adequate description of this clique. Nothing was sacred. They joked about anything and everything. After dating the Crow for some time, I was named "the Young Chick." From an early age, I was given credit for having a thick skin, which I must say served me well. In fact, I am sure that the skin took on a new layer to give added protection from the constant capers of this group.

As time went by, I became infatuated with this man, his cronies, and all the excitement this generated. Before long, he asked me to marry him. Of course, the rowdy friends were delighted with this news, because they could now take their kidding and joking to a new level. One of the stories they circulated throughout the town went something like this: "Did you hear about the 'Young Chick' calling her mother in South Georgia to tell her about the 'Old Crow'? She called her mother and said she was getting married to this man who was thirty years older than her, and her mother said that was fine. She then said that he was Roman Catholic. Her mother said that was fine. Finally, she told her mother that he was chairman of the Republican party for Richmond County. Her mother fainted." Everyone enjoyed this story at the time because in those days South Georgians thought being Republican was a fate worse than death.

The idea of marriage and a family had always been alien to "Gentlemen Husband," although this circumstance couldn't keep him from giving unsolicited advice to other men about how to manage their wives and children. Later I would learn that he had at times made remarks such as "Don't let those women tell you what to do. If she needs a ride somewhere, tell her to take a Yellow (referring to a taxi), or if there is a fire at the house, let her call the fire department, or if there is a burglar in the house, tell her to call the police. Just tell her not to bother you while you are over here at the club trying to play cards, golf, etc. Make those women understand that they should learn to handle their own problems."

When I approached my boss, the Gentleman Doctor, with the news that I would be getting married to one of his acquaintances, he took a deep breath and told me that he thought the guy was a really nice person. He went on to warn me, though, that he was concerned about his "rough" friends. No matter: I felt that I could handle the situation, so I pressed on with the wedding plans.

On June 24, 1961, we were married in a private ceremony at Sacred Heart Catholic Church in Augusta. A private ceremony was absolutely essential to guard against the friends who might truly make the marriage ceremony a joke of sorts. The first part of the honeymoon was to be in the mountains of North Carolina, and the second part was to be at Saint Simons Island, Georgia. If I knew nothing else about the game of golf, I knew emphatically that it took up a lot of his time. I learned that there was to be some previously scheduled golf with some men and women we were meeting on the second part of the honeymoon. Did I think it a little out of the ordinary to have my husband involved with golf games on our honeymoon? Not really.

Did I think it a little out of the ordinary to have my husband involved with golf games on our honeymoon? Not really.

Gentleman Husband

By this time I was aware that golf was simply a way of life with these people. It was also starting to dawn on me that maybe I should think about learning how to play this game so that I would someday be able to fit in.

After we returned from our honeymoon, we settled in at our new home—a small apartment about a block from the Augusta Country Club. The apartment number was 2B. Naturally, my husband chose to make a joke about this on every occasion possible. For example, when he was giving directions to someone about finding the place, he would always say, "It's apartment 2B, you know, as in 'to be or not to be.' " Given the difference in our ages, people thought this was an appropriate joke. He and his buddies never passed up the opportunity to joke about anything. What interested him most about this place was the close proximity to the club, where he and his friends enjoyed golf, as well as lots of bridge and gin rummy. Storytelling was his forte, though, and he spent long hours entertaining different groups of guys with his interesting jokes and yarns.

In August 1962 we had our first child—a daughter, Lee. This gave reason for another round of jokes and stories to circulate through the town about "the Old Crow" and "the Young Chick." A few months after Lee was born, I decided I would prevail upon my husband to buy some golf clubs for me. He did not seem thrilled with the idea.

Gentlemen Only

He remarked that most women don't play very well and in his words, "They can't even crack an egg"—meaning they could not hit the ball very hard or far. One Sunday night he came home a little later than usual from the club and, with a gesture of disgust, tossed a golf bag with clubs in the middle of the living room floor. "Here they are, but you will never be able to hit 'em" was his proclamation. Like never before, I was suddenly determined to learn to play the game of golf and to play it well.

⌒

Lee:

*D*ad was fifty-six when I was born as the eldest of what would be three daughters. I'm pretty sure that when he was asked to join the Augusta National, it was the first time a member had children—not grandchildren—as young as four years old with another just a month old and a third still two years away from birth. I'm also sure I was one of the few kids to literally grow up as a member's child at Augusta National, since the average age of a new member was around fifty.

As I've grown older and lived many places—both North and South—I have learned that being a member, or member's daughter, at Augusta means many things to many people. The one consistent belief is that it is one of the finest golf courses in the world and that the Masters Tournament is considered one of, if not the, premier tournaments in the world. Outside of those two realities, a membership at Augusta has varying levels of importance.

Dad was asked to join because he built strong relationships with several of the members—one of them being Jerry Franklin, a founder of the club. It also helped that Dad was such a dynamic and fun person who never offended anybody. Dad was always the life of the party. He was the person who always knew an entertaining story or joke. Still, it wasn't the content of his tales that stood out; it was his delivery. Almost every person who encountered my father described him as a real character. He was a Southern Gentleman's version of William F. Buckley. His accent and vocabulary resonated with a world gone by—when one spoke with proper English and could always craft a well-written letter. Most attorneys are quite adept at using the English language, and Dad was a master of decorum to boot. We learned at an early age the importance of being a good conversationalist and a clever writer. In my father's opinion, the most unforgivable trait one could possess was to be dull. And dull he was not. I often thought it was one of the reasons he was a well-liked member at Augusta. You always knew you could have an interesting, entertaining time with my father.

Robbie:

Plans for me to take up golf were put on hold because it was time to move into a new house, which, likewise, was a short distance from the Augusta Country Club, nestled in a subdivision appropriately named Country Club Hills. This proximity to the club enabled my husband to continue his club activities without letting domesticity intrude on his pleasure. Our second daughter, Cecelia, was born in 1966. Our family was completed with the birth of Sara in 1968, giving the females in our household a commanding 4-to-1 edge over the male. Occasionally, we opened our home to male dogs just so my husband would not feel too overpowered.

Our third move was to a residential area near our children's school. The fact that our new house was far away from the Augusta Country Club didn't have much of a negative effect on "the Old Crow" because now he had a new "love" interest when it came to the country-club set—and setting. In April 1966 he was asked to become a member of the Augusta National Golf Club, just a stone's throw away.

Gentleman Husband

Lee:

My father was not a typical Augusta member. He was not a baron of Wall Street nor was his net worth reported on the Forbes 400 list each year. He wasn't a board chairman or president of a major corporation, and he wasn't the heir to a multigenerational fortune. His last name couldn't be found on a household brand such as members named Firestone or Goodyear (tires), Ritz (crackers), Searle (Pharmaceuticals), and Doubleday (books). There were many times we joked with Dad as children that he was granted membership the year they graded on a curve. I often wonder what it would have been like to be one of the children of a "typical" member. Would my father's membership have had such a special influence and place in my life, or would it have been just another club on a long roster of playgrounds of the rich and powerful? If I had grown up as the offspring of a non-Augusta member, my immediate world as a child and teenager may have been very different.

My first real memory of being "a Member's Daughter" was perhaps triggered as a result of it being captured on an eight-millimeter-film home movie. It was Easter Sunday, April 1966, which also happened to be "Masters Sunday." A young upstart golfer by the name of Jack Nicklaus was on the leader board going into Sunday's play to voraciously chase the small white ball. I, on the *other hand, was already "making the turn" on my own chase for the white ball—in the form of Easter eggs. The home movie shows a jubilant four-year-old, dressed in frilly pink layers, with an enormous intricate basket laced with pastel satin ribbons. Each egg I discover under our vibrant azaleas is marked with equal enthusiasm. My father is standing nearby, smiling at me while preening in his crisp, new green jacket—the signature of membership at Augusta National—as my mother teeters nearby, nine months pregnant with what would become my first sister.*

3 *Gentlemen Golf Professionals*

Or, "Finding where the ground is"

Now that my husband had gained membership to golf's holy grail and with my decision to make childbearing a thing of the past, I figured it was time to retrieve out of the closet the golf bag that had been tossed in my direction and cursed with the proclamation of "Here they are, but you'll never be able to hit 'em." It was indeed time to prove my husband wrong and to not only take up this crazy game, but to make a real effort to excel at it as well. Maybe that hand-eye coordination that had proved so helpful at baton twirling would translate to some level of mastery for what was quickly becoming a family-wide passion. The idea of getting the hang of golf would seem more and more attractive as the marriage wore on.

Even with plenty of incentive to prove something, I quickly came to realize that learning to play the game of golf beginning at age thirty, while attempting to raise three children, was more than a little ambitious. My saving grace was the fact that I had no idea just how difficult the game could be. Being genuinely ignorant made it easy for me to become successful at something totally foreign to me. I wouldn't be predisposed to failure. Then again, I was smart enough to know that I needed to get as far away as I could from anyone who might know me or have reason to suspect what I was trying to accomplish, including, of course, my husband. I decided then and there to take up the game on the sly, and was curious to see where my secret mission would take me. Little did I know.

To accomplish this Mission Possible, I sneaked off to the outskirts of town, where I spotted a driving range that at one time had been a drive-in theater. The owner-operator was an elderly former professional baseball player with some golf knowledge, and he agreed to undertake the duty of introducing me to the game. I would get there in the morning before anyone else had arrived. The place would be deserted, which was one good reason for my being there at that time. I would go alone on these trips because it wasn't a social event for me, just another item to be crossed off my shopping list I took with me when I left the house. Grab the clubs and go.

By this time, Lee was about six years old and Cecelia two. Had it not been for my baby-sitter, Thelma, none of this would have been possible. Thelma was a mother's dream baby-sitter, a loving, funny, and entertaining woman whose caring manner gave me the security of knowing that I could leave home for hours without worrying about impending disasters back at our house in the Country Club Hills subdivision of Augusta.

Gentlemen Only

Lee:

I now realize that becoming a "member's daughter" at such a young age made me look upon this "distinction" with great casualness. I took for granted the easy access to one of the finest golf clubs in the world. Even though my first golf lesson occurred at the age of five, I never really viewed the National as anything more than another golf course—until I was in my teens.

I'm quite certain that my situation was a bit unique. First, my father was a bachelor until age fifty-five. He had never been married, and he lived at home with his parents until he met my mother, thirty-one years his junior. Dad didn't live with his parents because of any dependency issues. It was purely because it was inexpensive and afforded him all the luxuries he needed as a single man-about-town. When it came to a future wife, he was very picky. He was seeking perfection, and he found it in my mother. She was the ultimate trophy wife before the term became fashionable. Smart, clever, a great cook, and a devoted mother and wife, Mom realized at an early age that nothing would alter the lifestyle my dad had led for more than a half century—not marriage, not children, not tuition, not sickness, not graduations. She overcompensated and created the perfect home for her husband and kids.

Robbie:

My sole mission in making these excursions was to learn to play golf well enough to play golf with my husband. It was not something I discussed with friends or neighbors, or my husband. I had no concern about what the weather was like that particular day, and it was of little significance to me that the practice range had little grass and that the practice balls were dirty, scuffed-up "walnuts" better suited for throwing at pesky critters than pitching at flagsticks.

My first instructor wasn't a PGA-certified pro, either, but he was an extremely kind, driving-range owner who knew enough about the nuts and bolts of the golf swing to get me started on the right track. Part of his interest in seeing my golf game develop came out of his genuine sympathy for my golf ignorance. Later I learned that he had a daughter who at one time had been a pretty good golfer, only to suddenly quit the game to pursue other interests. Because he was no longer busy with his daughter, he was able to devote some of his spare time to helping me get started with the basics. I'm sure he felt that he had some unfinished business at hand and that I would be the one to take over where his daughter had left off years earlier.

So there I was with a golf teacher whose nickname was "Skip" and whose classroom was a run-down public driving range. I was on my way to achieving my goal.

Skip didn't burden me with lengthy explanations about the difference between pars and bogeys or pronation versus supination, and he didn't waste any time dissecting the tedious aspects of golf rules or any other complicated aspects of the game, of which there are many, to be sure. This was wise of him, operating in the Keep It Simple, Stupid mode. For that, I will forever be in his debt. I never would have made it past those little sessions if he had treated his golf instruction as rocket science or brain surgery. Instead, he simply told me to learn only one thing— "where the ground is." To ensure that I understood what he was trying to get across to me, he would take a bucket of his scuffed-up, dirty golf balls out into the hitting area and proceed to bury them among the tall weeds. Then he would step aside and simply say, "Now, hit 'em!!!!" How do you hit something that is barely visible? But that was the whole point of his hands-on instruction—to give me some basic tips and then let me flail my way out of the wet paper bag, so to speak. This was learning by doing, and it paid off.

So there I was with a golf teacher whose nickname was "Skip" and whose classroom was a run-down public driving range. I was on my way to achieving my goal.

30

Skip believed that for most women golfers, particularly beginners, their greatest difficulty when it came to learning how to swing the golf club was "finding the ground"; that is, being able to compensate with the stance and swing in such a way as to be able to hit the golf ball from any lie, whether on closely cropped fairway grass, in the sand, or among the weeds. Over time I spent hours on end just hitting those ugly driving range balls out of those weeds, and the drudgery paid off. I began to hit the ball pretty well, and Skip even admitted that, with lots of practice, I could become an average-skilled woman golfer, someone who could break a hundred and make a go of it in almost any foursome without embarrassing herself. And practice I did: Every single chance I got I slipped away from my household duties and children to practice this basic move of hitting out of the weeds. The next levels of the game never seemed as difficult as this first hurdle.

After many months of sneaking around learning the game, I decided to move to the next level and ask the golf pro at the Augusta Country Club to give me a lesson. I felt Skip had taken me as far as he could, and my appetite for learning the game was far from satiated. The Augusta Country Club pro, a Canadian native, had a reputation for being somewhat abrupt in manner but extremely knowledgeable about the golf swing. I was willing to compromise to achieve a greater end. He, however, knew little about speaking the King's English. After I got to the practice tee and hit a few shots under his watchful eye, he gave me some simple advice: "Turn them hips, Mrs. Heffernan!" which I added to "finding where the ground is" to form the foundation of what was to become my golf swing. Ben Hogan had his Five Fundamental Lessons, and now I was pleased as punch to have two I could call my own.

Still, it was obvious to me that most of my golf research was still in front of me—research in the form of books, magazines, and other periodicals containing detailed instruction about the proper swing. I had been careful to avoid written instruction earlier in my tutelage out of concern that too much information early on in the learning process would have been detrimental to my growth as a golfer. I have always believed that it is through hands-on experience, and trial and error, that a golfer can learn what is best for him or her. Now, by conducting research and experimenting with different things, I came to realize that I had wasted a fair amount of time trying numerous tips and advice that didn't work for me. Then again, all this was a necessary process for someone who knew nothing about building a proper swing sequence. Trial and error, remember? It works, as long as you are willing to look beyond the "wasted" time.

In taking up golf, I had no intention of becoming a club champion or even the Central Savannah River

Area (CSRA) champion, both of which I would ultimately accomplish. The CSRA is a region surrounding Augusta that includes other cities in Georgia and South Carolina. It was an effort made on the premise that I would be able to play in a husband-wife, mixed foursome, something which my husband frequently did. But my interest in the game grew, as did my desire to reach a level that went well beyond novice. It got to where, even when I was away from the driving range or a golf course, I would envision certain lob shots, playing out of the sand, or one of any assorted kinds of shots. I could even play shots over in my mind while on the floor of our den playing with building blocks with my children. Yes, I was attentive to my girls and loved playing with them, but the mental side of golf sometimes gave me a ready-made escape that would help relieve the occasional stress of child rearing. Our three girls would eventually take up golf at different ages and even take golf lessons, although some of the time they seemed more interested in caddying for their boyfriends than developing their own games.

Sometime after I started taking lessons at the Augusta Country Club, a friend told me about a professor at a small college in Aiken, South Carolina, who had proven to many to be quite adept as a golf instructor during his after-school hours. Indeed, his instruction was quite in demand.

I was able to work out a lesson schedule with him, and I discovered that his expertise was focused on pace and timing of the golf swing. He was the first person to talk to me about slowing the swing down and getting a sense of feel. Sequence was his big word. It was a long time before I knew the true significance of the word, but at the time it helped me form a better swing. The "professor" also taught me the importance of keeping a journal about the instruction I was

I was pretty much obsessive when it came to learning the golf swing, including a proper stance and body turn.

receiving. The professor's teachings came to me in reams of material, and I found it imperative to take notes so that I could continue working things out in his absence. It was through the professor that I learned about how an easy swing with proper body turn and follow-through could be so much more effective than a fast, off-balance swing that produces more frustration than power. All the elements of the swing and the game were starting to fall into place for

The follow-through is pretty important, too. But keep that head down through contact.

When I had to start giving Henry two shots a hole, I found it hard to make much use of the advice he gave me.

me. The lessons were paying off, and the golf course had become a fun place.

After three or four years, my husband learned about my interest and adventure with the game. Augusta is a small town where gossip is concerned, and those people who saw me taking a golf lesson at the Augusta Country Club were quick to ask my husband about it. They were eager to tease him about it. When my husband became aware of my taking golf lessons, he took it rather lightly. I think he thought I would be like most of his "women golfer" friends who played social golf. It wasn't that he discouraged me. He just never offered any encouragement. He knew I had become a passionate student about the game, although he stubbornly held on to the chauvinistic belief that I, as a woman, would never be a success at golf. I was as adamant as ever to prove him wrong, even though there were times I would become very discouraged about the whole thing. It was in those moments of mild despondency that I only had to remind myself about the curse: "Here they are, but you'll never be able to hit 'em."

Practice became my best friend. I became a junior-grade Ben Hogan with a philosophy of "not enough hours in the day to practice." Juggling children, gardening, and cooking in the mix with practice was a little tricky. The secret to my finding time for practice was cooking and doing chores at odd hours. When school was in session, I would try to find a little time to go to the practice tee.

Spare moments between car-pooling, baby-sitting, and peeling potatoes were filled with committing to memory whatever latest tip I had read or heard about. Sometimes I would just watch better players practice to see if there was a way to pick up something that I could use in my swing. One interesting observation about being a woman on the practice tee—hardly ever did a better player offer me advice, while all the hacker guys with a handicap of twenty or more were eager to help me with my swing. Go figure.

With all this practice under my belt, there was something happening inside my head and heart that I was unaware of at the time. The more I practiced and worked at the game, the more it took over my subconscious thinking. Before long, I would find myself on the way to the practice area, or the course, or to take a lesson, without having thought out my reason for doing so. It was almost like a calling, perhaps even an obsession, after a while. Without my realizing it, golf had moved in and taken over a portion of my life. It had established itself as my newest close friend. This was particularly true when things didn't go well at home with my husband or children. An upsetting chain of events would send me jumping into my car and heading for the companionship of my best friend, golf, in a heartbeat. Interesting game. By the time I returned from my practice session, the problem that sent me out of the house in the first place had worked itself out.

It was quite by accident that I learned how the swing isn't the most important element of the game. To my way of thinking, the greatest asset to be derived from playing the game is the strong friendship established between the aspiring golfer and the game itself. The difficulty of the game of golf dictates that an enormous amount of time and effort be spent on learning the game in order to play just an "average" game of golf. To play an even better game, not just average, a complete change in schedule is required. This is especially true with women golfers. With childrearing obligations and other household duties, finding time for the game was almost impossible. Still, even after I had attained my five handicap, I really had no idea what I had accomplished. I had unwittingly become a golfer better than about 95 percent of others who play the game regularly, as shooting rounds in the 70s had become familiar territory to me. For those keeping score at home, my lowest round ever was a 68 I shot at a golf course in South Carolina. Still, attaining a handicap of five meant a lot more to me than the 68.

The process of creating this better game of golf kept me so hypnotized that I didn't wake up to what I had done until other people started to be impressed with my accomplishment.

The process of creating this better game of golf kept me so hypnotized that I didn't wake up to what I had done until other people started to be impressed with my accomplishment. My husband, pretending to be unimpressed, would always make certain derogatory remarks like, "You shot 81 today. That's not too bad, but why did you have that seven on number five?" These kinds of judgments did not deter my work on my game, because I was under the spell of my best friend, golf.

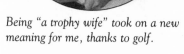

As time passed and I practiced harder, my husband actually started to play golf with me. Not that playing golf with him was pure bliss: He fell into that category of instructors who must be "tuned out." Most wives who play golf with their husbands learn early on to ignore the instruction they give on the golf course. Ignoring my husband's advice on the course became academic in my case, because when I began to give him two shots a hole and beat him, his advice became rather limited.

Being "a trophy wife" took on a new meaning for me, thanks to golf.

4 *Ungentlemanly Advice*

Or, "People don't like to watch women wrestle either."

The first professional golf tournament I attended as a spectator, ironically, wasn't played at Augusta National but at nearby Augusta Country Club. It was the Women's Titleholders Golf Championship, first held in Augusta in 1937 and won that year by Patty Berg. The major force behind the Titleholders was Dorothy Manice, a well-heeled New York native who lived in Augusta. She, along with many other interested people in town, spent a great deal of time and effort promoting the event. Even with all that support, however, the Titleholders never achieved a level of spectator interest satisfactory to tournament organizers, from its beginnings in the thirties until its denouement in the mid-sixties. Quality of play wasn't the problem. The eagerness of the leaders in town and among members at Augusta County Club wasn't a problem either. Lagging attendance at the Titleholders remained somewhat of a mystery throughout the tournament's existence, ultimately causing its demise. In retrospect, though, what the Titleholders organizers were experiencing in terms of lack of public support was no different than what many professional women's tournaments have experienced over the years. What was different about the Titleholders was that it happened to be held across Rae's Creek from a men's tournament well on its way to becoming the most prestigious annual golf event in the world.

By the sixties, interest in the Masters Tournament was growing by leaps and bounds, coinciding with my own introduction to and growing curiosity about the game. My interest was piqued even further when a friend asked me to accompany her to what would be my first Masters Tournament. This would be the only time I ever attended the tournament as a regular patron, parking in the public parking lot and walking with the large masses of ticket buyers to the course. This experience gave me an appreciation for the member's parking sticker that came later with my husband's inclusion in the club.

When my friend and I finally got to the front of the pro shop to pick up a program, my mind flashed back to the first time I had come here in my little white uniform to assist my doctor boss with Mr. Roberts's illness. The golf and the players did not mean very much to me that day, but the crowd and the production were overwhelming. In this glorious setting, I was now able to compare apples to oranges and understand why the comparative lack of interest in the Titleholders really was no mystery.

It didn't have the allure of the traditions, pomp, and pageantry of the Masters, and no Arnold Palmer or Jack Nicklaus strolling the fairways. This was a different world.

The story goes that shortly before the cessation of the Titleholders' last tournament in 1966, a last-ditch effort was made to revive the dying event. A rather influential citizen came up with the idea to breathe new life into the tournament by forming a "blue ribbon" committee to call on Mr. Clifford Roberts at the Augusta National and have him make suggestions as to how to improve the attendance at the ladies' event. The proper calls were made and the arrangements to have the meeting were completed. This committee spent long hours planning for their upcoming meeting with "the Wizard of Golf," fully expecting him to perform a miracle to revive their tournament.

This committee spent long hours planning for their upcoming meeting with "the Wizard of Golf," fully expecting him to perform a miracle to revive their tournament.

On the appointed day, the group met early at the Augusta Country Club to go over their notes and get everything in order for the big consultation. They probably knew that Mr. Roberts was a man of few words and very little patience. So it was to their advantage to have their questions and information in order for the meeting. As the car approached the gate at the National and proceeded down Magnolia Lane, there was an air of joyous anticipation in the hearts of each member of the "blue ribbon" group. Everyone just knew that the magic answer was only moments away.

The group was ushered into a room where Mr. Roberts was already seated. No time was wasted on life's little niceties or idle chatter. Feeling the impatience in the air, the spokesman for the group asked the big question: "Mr. Roberts, what do you suggest we do to improve attendance at the Women's Titleholders Golf Tournaments?" Before the group had time to get their pens ready to write, the answer came in a firm and authoritative voice: "You can't do anything. People don't like to watch women wrestle either." And with this terse answer, he pushed his chair back and left the group seated together, each with their mouths wide open.

Before the group had time to get their pens ready to write, the answer came in a firm and authoritative voice: "You can't do anything. People don't like to watch women wrestle either."

(It's too bad Mr. Clifford Roberts isn't around today to watch the LPGA at work. He would be surprised to find that even he can be wrong—way wrong—but also to see in action the adage "You've come a long way, Baby!!!!")

~

Gentlemen Only

Lee:

*S*ome of the happiest times in my early childhood occurred at the Augusta National in the summer months, when the club is closed. Most people don't realize that during the hot summer months, from late May until mid-October, the Augusta National completely shuts down for course and facility repair. A few select members, however, are provided a key to the front gate. My father was among those so fortunate.

On some late afternoons in the summer, we would pack up our station wagon with a great picnic lunch of chicken, salad, potato chips, Coca-Colas, and beer. We would also bring an elaborate array of fishing equipment, including Dad's tackle box and a fresh supply of crickets and worms. We would then pull up to the side entrance while Dad got out of the car and unlocked the gate. Mom would drive the car through the entrance while he relocked the gate behind us.

It was like we were entering another dimension. Traffic noises from Washington Road quickly faded into a quiet, velvet-like hush interrupted only by the distant chirping of the occasional bird. Even though we were the only people on the property, we felt compelled to whisper as if we were in a library. Once our senses adjusted to life within the gate, we drove around the curved road to the par-three course and the Eisenhower Pond, where we would set up camp until sunset. If there was only a little activity from the bream or bass in the pond, we would venture over to the pond on the par-three sixteenth on "the big course." During the Masters, I still get a kick out of seeing the reaction of those around me as I recount the thrill of "catching a big bream on number sixteen." Most longtime golf nuts think of Jack Nicklaus holing a long birdie putt at sixteen en route to winning another Masters when they picture the water-guarded hole, while my first thoughts of the hole begin with images of fish. When I tell others at the Masters about my fishing tales at number six-teen, their normally reserved, pinched faces suddenly turn into masks of horror as they spin their heads to scrutinize the source of such a comment! Once their eyes land on me, the gazes slowly drop down to the prominent club-house badge indicating member's daughter status. Those looks of disgust then melt away into a sort of foggy, rever-ent haze. It really was quite funny.

On one fishing expedition at the National when I was around five or six years old, I had my first encounter with the indomitable Clifford Roberts. During the summer, when the club was closed, it was not unusual to see Mr. Roberts out on the grounds, particularly around the par-three course. This very location and time of year would later be the venue for his unexpected suicide. On this occasion, back around 1967, I was busy building

sand castles in the bright white bunkers surrounding one of
the greens. No wonder: at this age, sand construction was
far more exciting than pulling in a reluctant bass. I
remember Mr. Roberts slowly walking down the hill in our
direction. I was frightened at this because we rarely
encountered another human out there while fishing, and I
didn't know what to expect, only that perhaps whatever I
was doing was breaking some rule. My first memory of
him was one of a stern, disciplined man whose focus
seemed somewhere else. He seemed polite to me, inquir-
ing about the layout of my amateur sand village and pro-
ceeding to converse with my father. All was well. Mr.
Roberts was one of the only men capable of inducing a little fear in my dad. Maybe it was that ever-present threat
of mysterious discipline on which the tenure of Dad's
membership rested. You never quite knew where you
stood, unless you fell below the expectation he had of you.
And those expectations and their accordant behavior were
very high.

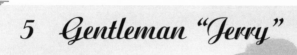

5 *Gentleman "Jerry"*

OR,
"WELCOME
TO THE
NEIGHBORHOOD."

I n the beginning, there was the Big Three, although most historians have focused only on the Big Two when it comes to how Augusta National got its start—Bobby Jones and Clifford Roberts. Actually, it was the Big Three, with local Augustan Jerome Franklin the third key link in the chain. Without this combination of men or the individual contributions of each of them, the Augusta National might not be what it is today.

My husband and "Jerry," which is what my husband called Jerome Franklin, had ties dating back to early childhood. They both grew up in the Irish, Roman Catholic neighborhood of downtown Augusta. At that time this neighborhood and its large families made up a rather significant portion of the city's population. However, the next generation of Irish evolved into professionals, businessmen, and successful entrepreneurs. The evolution was so complete that they further classified themselves into two categories, "Shanty" Irish and "Lace Curtain" Irish. Interestingly enough, I never heard any Irish refer to themselves or their relatives as being of the

"Shanty" variety. It seems that they did not even know anyone in that category.

Henry and Jerry remained friends as adults, although they weren't really close friends. Although Jerry continued to be a member of the Augusta Country Club, most of his time was taken up with his duties across Rae's Creek at the National. His reputation in Augusta as one of the Big Three made him somewhat of a hometown hero. I'm sure that in the back of my husband's mind was the thought that if he was patient enough and waited his turn, he would use this friendship to its fullest advantage someday. And sure enough, one day it came true.

My husband came home one day and told me in a reverent tone of voice, barely audible and quite nervously, that Jerome Franklin thought there might be a chance he could become a member. That is, if he performed certain duties to the satisfaction of the tournament committee. "Committee" was a term I found rather satirical when talking about the governing powers of that club. After all, everyone in the city knew that all decisions of any importance were made mostly by a single person— Mr. Roberts—not a committee. It did sound good anyway. My husband's performance skills were to be tested in the role as chairman of the transportation committee during the Masters. This committee was primarily responsible for obtaining courtesy cars, transporting them to the

National, and then issuing them to the players and VIPs who qualified for their use. The deal was that if he passed this test, then he might be considered for membership. It was like this was the interviewing process and if, upon review, you made a good impression, maybe the invitation would be considered. Lots of "ifs." Mr. Roberts wanted to make sure the prospective member would carry his weight and contribute something to the running of the tournament.

Given the close ties my husband and Jerry had, it was still somewhat of a battle to slide that green jacket past Mr. Roberts to anyone whom he had the slightest doubt about.

For the first time in his life, my husband became less than his own master. He served as the non-member chair of this committee for a year and then was asked to be a member the next year. I have seen it written many times that Jerome Franklin was chairman of the membership committee. Maybe??? I am not so sure. Given the close ties my husband and Jerry had, it was still somewhat of a battle to slide that green jacket past Mr. Roberts to anyone whom he had the slightest doubt about. The membership was offered and accepted, and it was a done deal in 1966.

Shortly after this time, we got a new neighbor across the street. Jerry and his wife moved in and we acted just

Gentleman "Jerry"

like all neighbors do, borrowing cups of sugar and all that. The best part about my husband and Jerry's friendship for me was later on when neither of these men played much golf, and the two of them would ride around in a golf cart at the National while I played with the guests we were entertaining. On such occasions as this, Jerry would relate some of the most unusual stories to me—just sitting out in the brigh shine, waiting for guests to arrive or whatever. One he asked me if I was aware that at one point in the there was a major renovation underway to have a l locker room in the main clubhouse. No way, I tho given that the ladies bathroom is closet sized. He was a fact. This is the true story:

It was a long time ago when the club had only bee open a short time and there were quite a few ladi who were wives of the northern members who play golf. Some of them did not play too well, but th played anyway. Among these ladies was an heiress the Jell-O fortune, Agnes. Agnes and Jerry's wife oft played a few holes together when Agnes came Augusta for a visit. It seems that on this particular da

53

Gentlemen Only

Agnes teed her ball up on number nine and shanked it into the cup on number eight. She screamed, "I just had a hole-in-one!!!" The two ladies continued their round. The next morning in the *Augusta Chronicle* sports section there was an article about Agnes's hole-in-one at the Augusta National. When Jerry got to the club, after reading the account in his morning paper, he had to pass by the workmen who were busy hauling in the bathroom fixtures from the putting green to complete the renovation for the ladies' locker room. He ran into Mr. Roberts in the front hall and decided he had better warn him about the newspaper article. So he explained that his wife and Agnes were playing golf the previous day when Agnes maintained she had had a hole-in-one. At that point in the conversation, Mr. Roberts said, "To hell you say!!She can't even hit it out of her shadow!!" With that, as Jerry explained, a loud scream came from the depths of Mr. Roberts's throat with the demand, "That's it! No ladies' locker room!!! Get all those fixtures out of here and there will never be a ladies' locker room at the Augusta National." End of story.

On my last visit there, that was certainly the case. I visited that same little closet area for my physiological needs. To this day Jell-O is not one of my favorite foods.

Gentleman "Jerry"

Augusta National's bunkers can be intimidating.

Lee:

As I met many people in my career and on my travels, I often encountered what can best be described as "the imposter member syndrome." Given that the membership was so small and so secretive, many people would casually throw out the proclamation that their father, uncle, grandfather, etc., was a member at Augusta. Since the membership was so small, I usually had a working knowledge of most of the names. I normally avoided telling most people that my father was a member—it would lead to a line of inquiry that often became monotonous or intrusive.

Gentlemen Only

When I encountered the imposter member syndrome, I usually let the person ramble on about the club, its members, and insider secrets—most of which were entirely false. One time, however, I couldn't resist busting someone. I was invited out to a hot new restaurant in New York with one of the vendors my company used. One employee of this vendor was originally from South Carolina and was quite full of himself. When he learned I grew up in Augusta, he immediately threw out that his "uncle" was a member at Augusta. I innocently said, "Oh, really," and asked his uncle's name. As soon as I heard it, I knew this guy was fibbing big-time. I knew his uncle wasn't a member. I let him go on and on about the Augusta National and the Masters—spinning tales that were so overblown.

Finally, I had a "final straw" experience. He began talking endlessly about how his uncle would take them out to play each year during their summer vacation. He continued on and on about the course, how it played, the flowers, etc. I finally had enough of this guy and asked him a few more specifics about his "summer vacation" on the course at Augusta—just to make sure he was set up for the fall. I then informed him that the Augusta National is closed from mid-May until late October and that no one is allowed through the gates except those members with a key—of which my father was one. I told the guy that I looked forward to telling my father that I met a fellow member's nephew and how extensively he spoke about the course. Needless to say, the "member's nephew" was quite silent for the balance of the dinner—which had the back-end benefit of making the other guests happier than I.

Among the many Masters Tournaments I got to watch, my favorite was the 1967 event featuring some third-round heroics by Ben Hogan, which I revisit later in the book.

6 Gentlemen on the First Tee

Or, "What's a Pretty Young Woman Like You . . .?"

Several years would pass before Cliff Roberts fixed his piercing eyes upon me once again—those eyes that had wanted information desperately. As one would expect, he had no recollection of our past meeting that involved the blood-letting.

The circumstances that led to our next meeting were rather unique. An old friend of my husband, Bob Wilson, had been accepted for membership at the Augusta National several years before my husband received his invitation. We were invited to a wedding and reception at the Augusta Country Club in the fall of my husband's first year of membership. Upon arriving at this particular event, we ran into Bob and his wife, Dorothy. The conversation finally got around to golf and my husband's new membership, which prompted me to say, "Dorothy, we will have to get the guys to have us out for a round at the National." With this comment, Bob went pale and became noticeably nervous. Dorothy replied, "Gosh! Robbie, I did not think women could play at that course." Bob quickly admonished me by saying he had tried to keep it a secret from Dorothy

Gentlemen on the First Tee

Entertaining guests at the Augusta National was a nice privilege that my husband enjoyed, including times when I was one of those grateful guests.

ever since he had become a member. However, Dorothy was ecstatic about going for her first outing there.

My husband told them the story of his first encounter with Mr. Roberts after being accepted for membership. On meeting him in a hallway at the clubhouse, my husband explained to Mr. Roberts about his wife's newfound love of the game. Mr. Roberts's words were, "Henry, we will be glad to have your wife play golf any day of the week, at any time she chooses, and as often as she likes. The only stipulation is the same as all other guests. She must be accompanied by a member if she is on the property here." Unlike certain courses that do not allow women at all, or some that allow them to play on certain days or at certain times, the National covers that problem by having wives categorized as "guests."

~

Lee:

There were only about twenty-five local members allowed at the Augusta National. It was a common joke that in order for a new Augustan to be considered for membership, another local would have to die or lose his membership—then his "slot" could be filled.

~

Robbie:

After Dorothy was assured that it was all right to go out there, we made the arrangements to meet there the next day, Sunday, at one o'clock. Everyone was aware that Mr. Roberts was in the "house"—meaning that he was on the property to watch everything taking place. With this in mind, Bob hurried us over to the tenth tee, after we teamed up with our caddies. He had observed that Mr. Roberts and his group were on the first tee, and he wanted to be sure to avoid any criticism by the club's notorious ruler. Over the years, Bob had taken great care to avoid any controversy that might endanger his membership. The scenario that took place between the first and tenth tee was not on Bob's agenda. As we started toward the tenth tee, my husband abruptly turned and headed straight to the first tee, straight toward the Roberts group.

Given my youth, novice-caliber golf expertise, and well-groomed appearance, my husband was always eager to introduce me to anyone who might be impressed with his "catch." He interrupted the conversation of the group of men, and said, "Mr. Roberts, I would like for you to meet my wife, Robbie." Without even a lift of his hat, a blink of his eye, or any change of facial expression, Mr. Roberts asked the question many before him had wanted to ask, "What's a pretty young woman like you doing married to such an old man?" I replied rather abruptly, "Well, Mr. Roberts, I just happen to like antiques!" He retorted, "Well, you sure as hell got one!" Because I did not want him to have the last word, I impulsively said something to the effect that he was in the right age group to identify an antique. There were a few chuckles in the group on the tee, and we moved off to the tenth tee where Bob waited, holding his breath. He had not been able to hear the conversation between Mr. Roberts and me, but he was sure there must have been something to fret about, considering the startled reaction in the crowd. Of course, Bob was more than a little uneasy about the exchange.

We completed the round of golf without further problems and there was no recall of green jackets—much to Bob's relief.

Henry sporting his green jacket after a round of golf.

7 *Gentleman Color-blind Member*

Or, "Ask any man in a green coat . . ."

GOLF TIP:
THE MAIN IDEA OF THE GOLF SWING IS THAT THE CLUBHEAD HITS
THE BALL AS A RESULT OF THE PROPER SEQUENCE OF MOVES BY THE
WHOLE BODY. YOU MUST TRY TO SWING SMOOTHLY, AND WITH THE
CORRECT TIMING. FORCE DOES NOT PLAY IN THIS GAME.

A few days after our golf game with the Wilsons, I got a call from Dorothy. She wanted to know if I had time to come by her house for a few minutes. She wanted to show me a letter that she figured would be very interesting to me because of my recent first-tee encounter with Mr. Roberts. The Wilsons lived a short distance from us, and I wasted no time in getting over there. I could hardly wait to see her secret letter.

Dorothy was well-known in the town for her artistic talent, and she had a reputation for being academically smart as well as gifted in a creative sense. She was always trying to improve situations she found lacking in proper function or beauty. There was never a dull conversation with her. So I knew whatever she wanted to share with me would be interesting and exciting.

When I reached the Wilsons' front door, Dorothy was waiting for me with the door open. We moved into her back den and sat down at a small card table. "Before I show you this letter, I need to give you some background on the facts," she said. So she related the following story:

Gentleman Color-blind Member

For years Bob had been afflicted with red-green color blindness. Every year when the two of them went to the Masters Tournament, Bob, wearing his green coat, would have some difficulty reading the Masters scoreboards, where red numbers indicate below par and green numbers above par. He would, for example, ask Dorothy, "Is that a red 4 or a green 4 on the scoreboard on hole No. 1?" It was the kind of question about the scoring he would ask time and again throughout the day.

After some years of this daily tournament questioning passed, Dorothy decided that she had had enough and decided to make a suggestion to the National about how to improve the scoreboards so that someone with Bob's problem could easily read the numbers from a distance. She set about doing her project in her usual fashion. She thoroughly researched the subject and compiled data to prove her point. Her final report revealed that she had consulted many experts, read volumes of printed matter, and compiled figures to substantiate her rationale. Her main discovery: A significant number of people are afflicted with red-green color blindness.

After much soul-searching, Dorothy decided to send a letter along with the results of her extensive research to Clifford Roberts. Her main concern was that she must keep this a secret from her husband, Bob, because if he found out, he would probably get hysterical. Everyone in the town, including Dorothy, knew how protective Bob was about his membership at the club. Sending Mr. Roberts a letter to suggest anything would never be on Bob's agenda—especially a letter of suggestion about those scoreboards. Every member knew how proud Cliff Roberts was of this apparatus, an invention of his own brilliant mind.

Dorothy summoned up all her courage and mailed the report to the Augusta National and did not tell anyone. She included her charts and statistics about color blindness. She even included her remedy for the problem—scoreboards with dark and light numbers on contrasting backgrounds. For example, a dark number on a white background or a white number on a dark background would be easy for color-blind persons to see. She further explained that television pictures would improve with this type of contrast. She signed the letter Dorothy Wilson, rather than Mrs. Bob Wilson, so that her husband's identity wouldn't be so obvious, perhaps even ignored. She was honestly trying to make the situation better, rather than seeking any self-gratification. A few days after mailing these facts, figures, and statistics to the National, she received a short letter from Mr. Roberts.

So ended Dorothy's background on the story. Well, that letter was lying on the card table in front of us. She said she thought I would like to see it since I had just had my encounter with Mr. Roberts on the first tee, and knowing I would get a big kick out of it. Which I did. In his response Mr. Roberts stated that the scoreboards were his creation and were so well designed that no improvement was necessary. He went on to say that if she had any problem reading the numbers in the future, she (assuming she was the one with the problem) should just "ask any man in a green coat for help."

Dorothy was so angry at this response that she tore the letter into small pieces and threw it into the trash can. Then she began to see the humor in all of this and quickly retrieved the pieces, glued them back together, and waited for the right moment to show the letter to her husband. She knew that even he would see the humor in this reply.

Then she began to see the humor in all of this and quickly retrieved the pieces, glued them back together, and waited for the right moment to show the letter to her husband. She knew that even he would see the humor in this reply.

As the years went by, Dorothy continued to go to the Masters with her husband, Bob, who was dressed in his green coat. Bob continued to ask Dorothy about the red and green numbers every year when he could not make out the color on the scoreboard. Most of the time Dorothy would help Bob with his dilemma, but sometimes she could not resist the urge to suggest that he might just "ask any man in a green coat—that is, if you can determine the color of his coat!"

⁓

Lee:

One of the funniest aspects of being the daughter of an Augusta National member was the effect it had on men. I realized the depth of this "aura" when I was in college. I graduated from Salem, a small women's college in Winston-Salem, North Carolina, which also is home to Wake Forest University, a school well known for some of the great golf alumni it has produced, including Arnold Palmer, Jay Haas, Scott Hoch, and Curtis Strange.

There were several fraternities on campus prominent for their golfing brethren. Frequently, a "flock" of Salem girls would head out to attend some of these fraternity parties at Wake Forest. On one of my first visits as a freshman, a girl-friend casually mentioned to a Kappa Sigma brother that I was from Augusta and the daughter of a member of the National. What followed reminded me of the old E. F. Hutton advertising campaign where a crowd would be suddenly silenced by the mention of the name. "Well, my broker is E. F. Hutton, and E. F. Hutton says . . ." The *revelation of this valuable information that there was an Augusta National member's daughter in this golfing fraternity house set off a quiet hush around the room, with all eyes riveted on me. By the end of the evening on one of my first visits, I had two marriage proposals and more male interest than I ever wanted. I learned after years of similar experiences to keep the "member's daughter" information as quiet as possible until I knew that I had interest in the male target.*

In 1991, more than ten years later, I had my male target. I had been divorced five years and was working at Turner Broadcasting. I was introduced to a CNN "hot-shot" on whom I immediately formed a huge crush. He truly was my ideal man at that time. To say this guy was cocky was an understatement—but, strangely, that was part of the appeal for me. I learned that he was a big sports fan, so I thought I would use the ultimate invitation to enable me to spend some time with him. I called and invited him to the 1991 Masters as my guest. We ended up dating for a while until geography (he had moved to L.A.) and career priorities got in our way. Oddly enough, ten years later, we reconnected and are engaged to be married. The "member's daughter" ultimately landed her dream man by playing the Masters card.

Lee and her four guests in the members' parking lot adjacent to No. 10 tee.

8 Gentleman Developer from Tennessee

Or, "I ain't playing golf with no woman!"

"I ain't playing golf with no woman!" shouted the rather large man as he lounged on the king-size bed in the motel room. "I ain't never played golf with no woman in my whole life and I ain't starting now. All women do is get out there on the course and hold everybody up and they can't hit a lick at a snake."

The Big Man glanced repeatedly at his diamond Rolex watch while he shouted these remarks, as if he had already started wasting his time here in the city of Augusta, Georgia. This big-time developer from Tennessee was accustomed to having his way and having it pronto. The other men—a kind-natured doctor and an older businessman—tried to calm the big guy down, which turned out to be out of the question. It seems getting his way with people was what he understood and the only thing he understood.

The three men from Tennessee had made a special trip to Augusta to play golf at the Augusta National as my husband's guests. A problem arose at the last minute when Henry had to attend to a rather important legal case on this first day that these men were scheduled to play golf at the National. My husband's contact and friend in this group was the older businessman, whom he called with a detailed explanation of his dilemma. My husband ended the conversation by suggesting they could play that first day of golf at the Augusta Country Club. He further suggested that I play with them to round out the foursome.

I learned later that the other two gentlemen were not privy to the conversation being carried on by telephone between the older businessman and my husband. They could hear their friend mumbling some words into the phone, but they had to wait until the phone conversation ended to get the full story, which, basically, was a sting operation on the two of them. The older gentleman explained the situation to them, choosing to appease them by saying that he would make it up to them by being the martyr in the group and taking me on as his partner in the usual friendly games that occupy a foursome's time during an eighteen-hole round of golf. Thinking that this would be the easiest bet he had ever won, the big-mouthed developer accepted the terms of the wager. The deal was that the older man and I would play the two of them in a little twenty-five-dollar Nassau, provided we were given some strokes. "She's an older woman and probably has about a thirty-six handicap,"

pleaded my partner-to·be. Of course, he was just fooling the developer, because he knew better. He had already been told by my husband about my golf game as well as the fact that I was many years younger than he. After a great deal of pleading, begging, and negotiating, the three men reluctantly left the motel and headed for the Augusta Country Club, where I was to meet them.

⁓

Lee:

As I became more entrenched in my career, the role the Augusta National played in my life evolved as well. The fact that I had a career and a paycheck on which I heavily relied surely was a unique concept among the children of the members. I was not a trust-fund baby, nor did I inherit a powerful career.

We had a cartoon pasted on one of the cabinets in our kitchen when we were children. It read, "His idea of an austerity plan is drinking a cheaper brand of scotch." That pretty much summed up our childhood. We were raised with silk-stocking tastes on a small-town lawyer's salary. So as I moved onward and attempted to move upward, I tried to leverage my father's membership at Augusta as much as possible. I sometimes entertained clients from various jobs along my career path—particularly once I started working in television marketing. My father endured many horrible golf outings for my sake, which often positively impacted Ted Turner's bottom line. Many advertising clients were "buttered up" on the eighteen lush, serene holes at Augusta.

Once Dad reached his eighties and could no longer play, he became the "cart general," barking commentary, club usage, and putting instructions from his cart. He would patiently record the scores of each player and entertain them with at least one great story on each hole. Dad loved to watch great golfers play. But it was very taxing for him to watch the not-so-great golfers play. Sometimes when I would accompany two guests for a round, my father and I would "bow out" at the turn and retire to the clubhouse for several rounds of gin rummy—a penny a point, a nickel a game. Dad was a great card player and did not have a great deal of patience if you didn't give him a competitive game.

Robbie:

I arrived at the pro shop through the back entrance and noticed three strangers looking around at the items on display there. Right away I knew these must be the men my husband had asked me to play golf with in his absence. The largest man in the group was anxiously looking at his

Rolex and then at the door of the shop as if the person he was expecting was keeping him waiting without good reason. As I moved closer to the group, I overheard the older man say, "Well, you know she is an old woman, and I am the oldest in this group, so maybe we should have at least two more strokes a side." The big guy said something like, "Okay, okay, you're probably right. It's a deal."

I approached the group, introduced myself, and explained I would be playing golf with them since their game had to be canceled at the National. The big developer grew pale, started to mumble under his breath, and gave his friend a look of total disgust. At the same time, the older gentleman in the group gave me a big wink as if to say, "Be quiet about your golf game."

We made our way to the first tee, and I asked the gentlemen to hit first as I was still playing the part of "hack." After they had hit their shots, I knew that it would be important for me to hit an impressive drive to set the tone of the match. As my tee shot sailed by theirs on the fly, I heard the developer moan, "I have been had." And that was pretty much the way the match went, with my partner and me winning the front nine, back nine, and the overall eighteen. At one point in the match, the developer suggested to my partner that he (the older businessman) should just tee my ball for me and then watch from the cart, indicating that I was beating them by myself.

When it was all over and doses of humility had been parceled out, several dollars passed into my palm.

I love it when a plan comes together.

As we sat on the terrace of the clubhouse after the match, laughing and talking about the unfair match the older man set up for us, I noticed that the developer was no longer looking at his Rolex. On the contrary, he was totally relaxed and having a good time. He kept saying over and over, "I have never played golf with a woman, and I have never had so much fun getting beat." His companions said they could hardly wait to get back to Tennessee to tell all his friends about him playing golf with a woman—a woman who beat him, even without the strokes. Apparently, his reputation as a male chauvinist was well known in his hometown, and now word was spreading.

Apparently, his reputation as a male chauvinist was well known in his hometown, and now word was spreading.

The next day the three guys played the Augusta National, as planned, with my husband replacing me as the fourth. After completion of this round, the three men expressed their appreciation for getting to play at the National and said they hoped they could return the next year. And if they were invited to come again, they wanted to make sure that they could have the same match with me at the Augusta Country Club. So it became an annual outing for them and me. Every year the older businessman threatened to tell the Rotary Club back in Tennessee about this Rolexed male chauvinist who came annually to lose a three-way Nassau to "the little old woman."

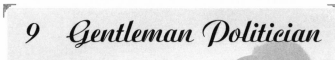

9 Gentleman Politician

Or, "How many holes do you need anyway?"

B amboo provides an excellent obstruction for almost anything it is planted around, between, or near. In fact, the mere mention of bamboo to the average person and their first comment is, "That stuff will take over." That is exactly what Cliff Roberts hoped to achieve when he planted bamboo around the property of the National.

When riding along Washington Road, a person is unable to get even a glimpse of what is behind the aggressive stand of bamboo that runs along the side of this thoroughfare. Bamboo and other plants, trees, and shrubs are placed there to hide anything that surrounds the course, anything that would suggest to the person inside the property that there is another world out there. Once you are inside the property, you are lulled into thinking that there really isn't anything outside this heavenly world. The only place that Mr. Roberts was unable to screen completely from view was the ninth hole at the Augusta Country Club. Amen Corner comes so close to this other course that there isn't room to plant a complete screen on the property the National owns. And, of course, the

Augusta Country Club keeps its side of the property line totally clear of obstructions to the view, in order to see into the private world of the National. The patrons sitting in the stands behind number twelve tee during the Masters Tournament are able to see golfers playing the ninth hole at the Augusta Country Club. I have heard that Mr. Roberts would become extremely upset when he overheard someone in the crowd ask, "What is that golf course over there?" It was a problem about which he could do nothing, because the club across the way was there long before the National was built.

Rae's Creek runs in front of number twelve and along the side of number eleven. Given the problems this little waterway has caused professional golfers over the years, the television coverage of the area, and all the material that has been written about it, the creek is practically a household word. What the average golf enthusiast doesn't know is the debate that has taken place over the years about the property around this stream. Flooding during heavy rainstorms wreaked havoc with the fairways and greens at the National. With a great deal of money and clever engineering, the club was able to solve its problem. That was not the case for residents downstream. City and county officials were called to the scene of flooding numerous times before they decided to correct the problem for those homeowners affected by this problem.

Politicians were always reluctant to approach the National about anything controversial. Because of all the benefits the community and surrounding areas derived from the tournament, no one wanted to upset the apple-cart—not to mention the problem of dealing with Cliff Roberts. However, the problem became so bad that something had to be done. City and county officials determined that an extension drainage system was needed to correct the flooding problem. This plan made it necessary for the Augusta National and the Augusta Country Club to give a little land to help the engineers install the proper equipment.

About this time, the Masters Tournament committee decided they needed more land along the hidden side of Rae's Creek in order to move the tee back on number eleven. Their aim was to make the eleventh hole longer and more of a challenge for the tournament contestants. The Augusta Country Club was also having a problem with flooding on their eighth green. And as I have said, the upscale residents downstream were up in arms about the flooding. The convergence of these situations in which everyone had a vested interest made it necessary to call a meeting to solve the dilemma.

The convergence of these situations in which everyone had a vested interest made it necessary to call a meeting to solve the dilemma.

The meeting included representatives from the Augusta National, the Augusta Country Club, and home-owners, as well as the county and city politicians. The person in charge of the meeting was "Mac" Parsons, who had been elected to the board of county commissioners so many times that he practically controlled the agenda of meetings. He represented the section of Augusta that was at the opposite end of the social spectrum from the attending members of this meeting. He was widely known to be rather outspoken, never letting his middle-class background or social status keep him from expressing his opinion. Timid he wasn't. Rounds of golf that took hours and social functions that interfered with politics were left off his calendar completely. Not only did he decline to participate in these kinds of things, he had limited knowledge of anything relating to them. USGA meant "Us Georgians" to his way of thinking.

As the meeting wore on into the night, it was painfully obvious that there would be little success in solving everyone's problem. Because the Masters Tournament brought so much revenue into the city and county, the burden of acquiescing most assuredly would be placed on the Augusta Country Club. And so that group of representatives had to hold firmly to "their ground," both literally and figuratively. As the clock approached the midnight hour, and after hours of fighting over the issues,

Mac, the quintessential politician, rose from his chair to take charge of the wrangling. In a loud and firm voice, he declared, "Gentlemen, we cannot continue to argue about this matter. We are only talking about a small bit of land needed for this sewer improvement, and the Masters club needs just a small strip for their purpose. We would only be taking some land from the eighth hole on the country club property. I fail to see where this would create a problem for that course. This would do away with just that one hole and, after all, they would still have seventeen other holes left on the course. Seventeen holes is still a lot of holes to play on. I just can't see where there is that much difference in seventeen or eighteen holes!"

The meeting ended abruptly with all sides shaking their heads in disbelief. The opposing sides agreed in whispers, after they assembled in the hallway, that they would be better off to reach an agreement on their own, then later advise the city and county of their arrangements.

There is a happy ending to this story. Neither course had to give up a hole and the flooding problem was solved without too much destruction on the peripheral banks of Rae's Creek. I have to smile every time I hear some television commentator discuss the perils of Amen Corner and Rae's Creek. They don't know half the story!

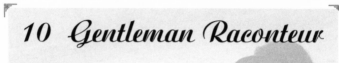

10 Gentleman Raconteur

OR, "JUST
HOW BIG
ARE THOSE
MOSQUITOES?"

It is a little-known fact that during the Roberts Regime, local members—that is, members from the Augusta area and close enough to drive to the club—were looked down on just slightly as second-class members of Augusta National. Cliff Roberts and other members from far away were often heard referring to the locals as "Trunk Slammers," a term that described the way they arrived to play golf. Most of the membership is comprised of men who have to fly into the city and come "down Magnolia Lane" in the limo or van provided by the club. Maybe there was just a little envy that these guys lived close enough to drive to the club almost anytime they chose. Another advantage, or at times a disadvantage, was the opportunity to entertain more guests on the golf course.

The most frequently asked question by anyone who plays golf, goes to the Masters, or just starts a conversation about Augusta is: How does a person get to be a member of the Augusta National Golf Club? Almost everyone knows that the selection for membership is by invitation, not application. But the next question is more difficult to answer: How does one get an invitation? The direct route in this time period was to have some contact with Cliff Roberts and have him be impressed with you. Because his health was less than perfect, he had occasion to come in contact with several local physicians. These physicians, like the Gentleman Doctor I wrote about earlier, could come away from a house call, or in this case a club call, with an invitation to membership at the National. That is, if they made just the right impression on the chairman of the club.

The local rumor mill has it that on one particular weekend visit, Mr. Roberts developed an acute urinary tract infection. When the urology group of choice was called, the doctor on call for the weekend was not the best golfer in the group of physicians, but rather an attractive, gentlemanly, mild-mannered man with some golf expertise. There was in this association of doctors a man with an excellent golf game, but it just so happened that he wasn't on call at the important moment. Therefore, he missed the opportunity of a lifetime, because the doctor who made the club call was offered membership almost instantly. Mr. Roberts was so very impressed with this

He missed the opportunity of a lifetime, because the doctor who made the club call was offered membership almost instantly.

doctor that he remained one of Roberts's personal favorites from that time forward.

Most times, Cliff Roberts's opinions about people and their character were right on target, but there was one flagrant error involving a local attorney, who later was convicted of fraud. Everyone is allowed some mistakes, even Mr. Roberts. But this one went too far. His assessment of this attorney and his close involvement with the man would prove a little embarrassing. The lawyer and

Lee and her dad had some nice father-and-daughter moments on the golf course, and he loved regaling her with stories in much the same way he did others.

Mr. Roberts were very close social friends outside the club. On some occasions Roberts was entertained in this member's home and would occasionally fly in the lawyer's private jet to exotic locations for dinner. Regardless, after the attorney's fraudulent business transaction became public, he had those strict disciplinary rules slapped on him as if he were an unknown individual rather than the close personal friend of the chairman. Roberts's rules were applied equally to everyone, even someone who might manage to get close to him.

There were no written rules for acquiring membership, but there were some subtle unwritten rules that applied under Mr. Roberts's reign. Some of his unwritten rules:

1. The candidate must play golf—not well, but he must know how to play the game.

2. The candidate must play cards—not well, but adequately, at least.

3. The candidate must behave in a gentlemanly and dignified manner at all times. (There cannot be any exceptions to this rule. There have been quite a few members kicked out for failing to conform totally to this rule.)

4. "Local members" or "Trunk Slammers" should be excellent raconteurs. (By possessing this talent, the locals could help entertain the members who had to fly in and stay on the premises of the National.)

The fourth unwritten rule is what got dear old "Fred" kicked out. Well, actually, it was a combination of Nos. 3 and 4, because the story he told that coincided with his getting into trouble was an excellent story. However, this particular story made him seem a little less than dignified in the eyes of the members present at the time, and that wasn't good.

Fred was the quintessential local member. He was an engineer, an honors graduate from Georgia Tech. He had played football, was an excellent tennis player and an avid hunter and fisherman, and he could play golf well. Those attributes by themselves made him excellent Augusta National material. Furthermore, he could tell a tale better than anyone, and this was his greatest talent. Because of his numerous talents and interests, he was able to recount an interesting tale about almost any subject that came up in casual conversation. A crowd was always around him when he was relating one of his personal experiences, or someone else's misfortune, or any kind of narrative that would entertain people. He had the unusual ability to take a very small event or happening and convert it into a saga of bountiful proportions. His slow, Southern drawl and deep-pitched voice lulled his audience into a state of nervous anticipation by the end of his stories. He could keep his listeners completely captivated and entranced for a longer time than most other raconteurs. Fred had only been a member of the National for a short time when the other members became aware of his expert story-telling talent. They were as mesmerized by it as the rest of the town.

The story goes that there was a "Members Only" tournament that took place on a cold Saturday morning in January, and the misfortune that befell poor old Fred took place that same day. It seemed that his foursome had played early and finished quite a while before the rest of the field completed play. The group retired to the men's grille to warm up by the fire and wait for the other players to come in. After several drinks had warmed the insides and a bright fire in the huge fireplace had warmed the outsides, Fred settled into a long round of joke telling. Those who were there say that Fred was really wound up by the time all of the other players finished and the dinner was served.

After several drinks had warmed the insides and a bright fire in the huge fireplace had warmed the outsides, Fred settled into a long round of joke telling.

Dinner was served in the area known as "the Trophy Room." This room is warmly decorated with a massive fireplace, lots of windows, bright colors, and fresh flowers everywhere. The only thing cold about this room comes from the eyes of the persons in the oil paintings hanging on the three surrounding walls. One set of these eyes belongs to Mr. Cliff Roberts, and the other two belong to Bobby Jones and President Eisenhower. When you are seated in this room, you always have the impression that these people are here in these paintings for the express purpose of maintaining good order and to see that the dignity of the place is preserved.

Old Fred, seated amidst all this pomp and circumstance, appeared to fit right in with the rest of the members. However, all the local members knew that he had one problem, and sometimes that problem had surfaced and become an albatross around his neck. Whereas he was an excellent businessman, talented golfer, and well-rounded athlete, his background left a little to be desired. It would not be fair to say that he was born on the wrong side of the tracks, but it was widely known that he did not spend his childhood in the upscale "Hill" section of town.

He had told so many stories that he realized that his inventory was getting low. So the conversation turned to the events surrounding a fishing trip he and his business friends took to the coast of South Carolina.

On this particular occasion Fred was seated at a large table in the Trophy Room with a group of members from the Midwest and the North. He had told so many stories that he realized that his inventory was getting low. So the conversation turned to the events surrounding a fishing trip he and his business friends took to the coast of South Carolina. After the story had gone on for some time, one of the members from Boston asked about the big mosquitoes that inhabit this part of South Carolina. His question went something like this: "Fred, I hear that there are lots of mosquitoes down there, and not just regular-sized ones, but really, really big ones." Fred's reply went something like this: "You got that right! Those mosquitoes are really, really big. You want to know just how big those buggers are? Why! They are so big, they can f— a fly!!!!" Supposedly at that point, the member from Boston was said to have fainted, and several members had to leave the room for air. The cold eyes of the men in the portraits must have closed in a moment of disbelief.

In just a few days, Fred had all the time in the world to fish and hunt. His green coat had been recalled along with his membership. Actually, his story about the sexuality of the mosquitoes had nothing to do with his dismissal. The real cause had something to do with bid rigging in the company where he was employed. So the rule, written or unwritten, at the National is that a member who is accused of any crime or misbehavior unbecoming a gentleman is automatically dismissed. Guilt or innocence has nothing to do with it. They do not wait for the slow-moving judicial system to establish guilt or innocence. Nothing is allowed to cast a shadow on the hallowed grounds that house the legend and legacy of the great Bobby Jones.

My husband and I on the hallowed grounds of Augusta National.

11 Gentlemen Caddies

OR, "THAT
SHO' IS A
LONG
DISTANCE."

GOLF TIP:
THE FOURTH OF SIX SENSES OF GOLF: SMELL—OKAY, SO NOT IN
THE LITERAL SENSE. SNIFFING AROUND FOR EVERY AVAILABLE
WAY TO IMPROVE THE SWING IS A MUST. READ, WATCH
INSTRUCTIONAL VIDEOS, STUDY THE PRO GOLFERS ON TV,
EMULATE GOOD LOCAL PLAYERS, ETC.

During the years I played golf at the Augusta National, mostly in the seventies and eighties, the old-time black caddies were more in total control—as least in control of their duties and their domain, versus the current-day caddies at the Augusta National. Even though some caddies from the past are still around, the unusual personalities aren't quite as obvious. Most people who were privileged to have one of these caddies carry their bag knew that these guys were unique in so many ways. They were a community unto themselves. There was a caste system of sorts, the language they spoke was a little different, and their personalities were distinct from one another.

The first time I enjoyed the pleasure of having one of these caddies carry my bag—or "tote" it as they would say—a new dimension was added to my golf game. After turning from Magnolia Lane into the parking lot in front of the pro shop, the car was literally attacked by the white-coveralled caddies. Usually, the pro had already alerted the caddie master about the member who was on his way and how many caddies would be needed to take care of him

98

The caddies at Augusta National add much to the golfing experience there, especially with their expert local knowledge.

and his guests. So the minute the caddies recognized the car coming down the drive—and they all knew what kind of car everybody had—they were ready to pounce on the bags in the trunk. This was followed by a brief frenzy as the player's equipment was assigned to the appropriate caddie. The caddies were always eager to impress in hopes of getting a nice tip at the end of the day.

After we went through the pro shop and proceeded to the first tee, the caddies came from the parking lot with the bags. I glanced at my clubs and realized that they had been cleaned by the caddie sometime between my getting out of the car and arriving on the first tee. It was easy to tell that these caddies do not just "tote" the bag; but they almost possess the person whose bag is on their shoulder. In other words, I could tell that my caddie felt like he "possessed" me, my clubs, and my decisions about the round. As we began walking down number one after hitting our tee shots, I started remembering some of the unique stories I had heard about these Augusta National caddies. One story had to do with their nicknames—they all called each other by some sort of personalized name like "Cemetery" and "Long Distance." Each nickname usually had a story behind it or a valid reason the caddie was assigned that name. In the case of "Cemetery," he supposedly was pronounced dead at some time in his past and while being placed in the morgue, he came back to life. The story behind "Long Distance" was that he was Sam Snead's caddie at some time and gave Mr. Snead too much club to hit on number 4, a par-three with a busy thoroughfare behind it. He not only gave Mr. Snead too much club, but insisted he hit that club because in the caddie's words, "That sho' is a long distance." Of course, Snead's ball sailed over the green, over the trees, and into the road or subdivision across the road. So from that moment on, this caddie was "Long Distance." These are only a few samples of the creative nicknames.

Gentlemen Caddies

Lee:

*T*he caddies at Augusta enjoy watching great players wrangle the taxing course as well. Often they would place bets among themselves after watching their assigned player's tee shot on number one. On those occasions when it was obvious that my guests would be joining the "century club" on the back nine, my dad would reward the caddies with a round of Transfusions at the turn. The Transfusion was a unique elixir of grape juice, ginger ale, and club soda.

Often caddies would be out partying into the wee hours the night before. Carrying a heavy golf bag under the warm Georgia sun in a dehydrated state made the Transfusion on number-ten tee a virtual mirage on the number-nine fairway. My father was notoriously cheap and would frequently yell out to the caddies as they climbed number-nine fairway to "enjoy a cold Coca-Cola," implying no Transfusions would be obtainable. Obviously, exceptions were made on those days when the performance of the players was more strenuous to watch than to caddie for.

Robbie:

*R*emembering back about that first round with these caddies reminds me of that frightening moment I discovered "the bet." Not the wager we had made in our group, but the bet the caddies had made among themselves on the first tee. Little did I know that it was standard operating procedure for the caddies to gamble among themselves, placing their bets on the person whose bag they were carrying. We were well into our round before I happened to overhear some of the conversation going on between two of the caddies. They were discussing their "horses"—that would be us—the persons whose bags they carried. It made me quite nervous to know that my golf swing had a price on it and that the money that might be lost was not mine. Concentration takes on a new dimension when you know you are someone's horse.

When we reached the first green, I never heard so much conversation and planning about how the putts would break and how hard to hit the putts. These four caddies had more opinions about those greens than I had ever heard before. I now realized that some of their concern had to do with their gambling. They not only had an overall bet on their "horses," but they had separate bets on the putting part of the round.

Everyone who knows anything about golf and the Augusta National knows about those tricky greens. These caddies knew more than anyone. One reason for their knowledge was that most of them grew up very near the course in a neighborhood that adjoins the property at one section. Augusta, like some other Southern towns, had a section that was predominately black. This area ran along the property lines of both the Augusta National and the Augusta Country Club. Consequently, as young adventurous children, the present caddies had sneaked over the fences to this property on a daily basis. While they were playing around, they were also learning the subtle breaks in those treacherous greens. This information would serve them well later on. It also served many golf professionals well when it came down to those last few crucial putts of the Masters Tournament.

As young adventurous children, the present caddies had sneaked over the fences to this property on a daily basis. While they were playing around, they were also learning the subtle breaks in those treacherous greens.

We completed our round that day without too much disaster, but I came away knowing that four players, four caddies, and the surroundings of this course made concentration on the swing more than a little difficult.

Sometime later, I learned that the caddies at the National had given my husband a nickname. To be given a nickname by them was certainly a compliment because it meant that you were due a certain amount of notoriety. My husband came by this nickname during the Nixon administration when the president put a freeze on hiring in the federal government. When the National opened in October of this particular year, the caddies were all lined up in an informal group near the pro shop. As my husband strolled by, he jokingly said to them something like, "We'd like to give you boys a raise this year, but you know the president has put a freeze on those kinds of things." The caddies were already aware that in the community he was known to be slightly tightfisted. Given his statement to them and his reputation, they came up with "Mr. Freeze" as a nickname for him. This moniker was not ever used on the grounds of the National, but in their own group when they would refer to him. Late one summer afternoon, my husband was in the passenger seat of my car as I took a yard-man back to his house in the black neighborhood. When we reached a certain area of this section of the town, we saw a large gathering of Augusta National caddies. Immediately, there was a loud chorus that went up from this group: "Hey!!! Mr. Freeze!!!" My husband tipped his hat to them

Immediately, there was a loud chorus that went up from this group: "Hey!!! Mr. Freeze!!!" My husband tipped his hat to them and nodded, as if to say, "Thank you, gentlemen, for making me part of your group."

and nodded, as if to say, "Thank you, gentlemen, for making me part of your group." I guess having a nickname denoted inclusion and status whether you were a caddie or a member.

My favorite caddie was a soft-spoken, all-business man whose nickname was "Blue." Blue had that unusual talent to make the golfers whose bags he carried feel like they could play better golf than they realized they could. In the protected environment of the National, with a caddie like Blue, everything was possible. In one round, Blue so hypnotized me that I was one under par after seven holes before I realized that I "couldn't" play that well. Blue and I respected each other so much that I never felt comfortable asking him the origin of his nickname. However I did ask one of his buddies when he wasn't there. His friend seemed shocked that I would have to ask and replied—"We call him Blue because he is so black that he seems blue." Anyway, color was not important to me. I just knew that Blue could bring out the best in my golf game.

His friend seemed shocked that I would have to ask and replied— "We call him Blue because he is so black that he seems blue." Anyway, color was not important to me. I just knew that Blue could bring out the best in my golf game.

There has been much written about Mr. Roberts's relationship with these caddies. It was common knowledge that he took very good care of them. I believe if he were still alive, there would still be only local caddies used during the Masters Tournament. When I watch the tournament now, I feel as though something is missing—it's the presence of these unusual and wonderful caddies. Not that they are entirely missing. When Ben Crenshaw won the Masters in 1995 for his second victory at Augusta, he used his longtime Augusta National caddie Carl Jackson, who had also carried Ben's bag when he won in 1984.

A few of the Augusta National's caddies at work.

Lee:

M y father had several clients from his law practice whom he would regularly entertain at the National. Typically, a guest would give the member some type of gift as thanks for the day of play. When asked by my guests what they should bring my dad, I would always advise, "Stay within the three key groups: scotch, tobacco, or chocolate." You could never fail in my father's eyes if you presented any one of these. My dad had one Japanese client who would sometimes bring two of his Asian guests to play at Augusta. I would often hear the stories of their experiences over dinner that night with our family. For most of these Japanese guests, playing Augusta was considered the pinnacle of their life experience. One guest even remarked to my dad at the end of his round, "Mr. Heffernan, I ready to die now."

Frequently, these guests would give my dad gifts from Japan. Since these gifts did not fall in one of the favored categories of scotch, tobacco, or chocolate, they would usually end up (and stay for long periods of time) in the backseat or trunk of Dad's car.

To say that my father was low-tech is an understatement—he never fully mastered the most basic television remote control. I, on the other hand, love high-tech gizmos of all kinds. One day I discovered by accident the Japanese stash in Dad's car. Here, randomly tossed on *the backseat, was some of the latest, hottest state-of-the-art Japanese equipment. One of these items was a tiny, Hi-8 camera. Its features included several that were not even available at that time in the United States, such as a color viewfinder and automatic playback. The challenge rested in the fact that all of the symbols (play, fast forward, etc.) were in Japanese characters. I snapped this up and tried to explain to Dad the value of what he had, but my zeal rested on uninterested ears. I remember taking it to a camera store. The owner was in awe of the fact that I had one of these cameras and quickly offered me forty-five hundred dollars for it. Eleven years later, I still have and use this Hi-8 camera.*

12 Gentleman Secretary of State

Or, "This is the Augusta National calling to invite you . . ."

"This is the Augusta National calling to invite you and your husband for cocktails tonight as the guest of Secretary of State George Schultz. He and some of President Reagan's staff will be here to meet you around six o'clock," the administrative assistant stated in a rather efficient tone.

I stared at the phone in disbelief. What made this invitation unusual was not the high-level political status of the hosts, but that there was a social function that included spouses. From the first day of my husband's invitation to join, he had been told emphatically about the unwritten rule that governed activities held in this clubhouse: no wedding receptions, no teas, no tennis, no swimming pools, and no other social functions of any other kind that would make one think of this as a regular country club. "This is a golf club, not a social club. It is to be used exclusively for that purpose." Words to live by if you are invited to become a member. Someone must have forgotten to explain this to the then-secretary of state, who was very outgoing and friendly. Having a crowd around when he and his Washington associates came for a golfing weekend did a lot

110

to rid the clubhouse of its tomblike atmosphere. Furthermore, the local members were thrilled and excited to be a part of this hosting process. Mr. Schultz was smart enough to realize that the dullness that settled over the National after the sun went down was not the kind of atmosphere he wanted for his guests.

> *Mr. Schultz was smart enough to realize that the dullness that settled over the National after the sun went down was not the kind of atmosphere he wanted for his guests.*

When we arrived that evening, the room was filled with a great deal of laughter and conversation. The whole place seemed to have taken on a warm glow, which is not a term often used to describe the club under any normal circumstances. Mrs. Schultz, Mrs. Bush, Mrs. Baker, and other wives of the important men introduced themselves as we entered the room where the party was held. President Reagan was not there on this particular occasion, but he did come down to Augusta at other times. Over in a corner, Donald Regan, the secretary of the treasury, was holding forth while the other men listened intently.

After a short while, Vice President Bush entered the room unannounced and with only a small amount of fanfare, adding even more warmth and conversation to the gathering. My first impression: Here is a really nice guy.

Gentlemen Only

As history has played out its hand, meeting Mr. and Mrs. Bush was one of my best memories of the National times. Even now as I watch their son perform his presidential duties, I am not surprised he does that so well. With parents like his as role models, failure would be difficult. I came away from these functions thinking maybe this was not a social function, but just a little like a patriotic duty. The Southern hospitality given by the local members might have helped lower the stress level of these Washington politicians.

Immediately following the cocktail party given by Mr. Schultz, most of the local members and wives went into the Trophy Room for dinner. Dining at the Augusta National is always a pleasure, whether it's a sandwich under the umbrellas outside or in the more formal surroundings of the inside dining room. There isn't anything special or unique about the china, silverware, or furnishings. It has more to do with the aura of the place created by what has happened there. I sometimes thought that maybe the food was just average, but because of where it was served, it had a special flavor. The person eating the food had to be so overwhelmed by the surroundings and the history of the place that the mind could play tricks on the taste buds. As often happened, the dinner conversation got around to my golf. The question came from one of the local wives who asked where I might be playing golf the next day. I replied that I would be playing in a church tournament on the municipal course, locally named "the Cabbage Patch" because of its poor conditions. The lady replied that she thought it would be difficult to go from the Augusta National to something like "the Patch." "Not at all," I said. In fact, I had learned to appreciate the challenge of the game of golf to the extent that where I played was of little or no consequence. Playing different courses, even those courses considered unattractive, was an opportunity to test my golf game, which I was constantly trying to improve.

∼

Lee:

This is the story of how Augusta National played a significant role in my career.

In 1986 I started work at the Georgia Railroad Bank in Augusta. A few days after I started work as advertising manager, First Union National Bank acquired Georgia Railroad. My boss instructed that we needed to spend the balance of our marketing funds for the year, but (1) we couldn't market our products because they would be changed with the merger, (2) we couldn't market our service because it left a great deal to be desired, and (3) we couldn't market our brand since the name would change within the year. My boss expressed an interest in trying to retain customers with all of the impending change and conversion, but left me with little to market.

At about this time, 1986, college basketball lost one of its greatest players, Maryland's Len Bias, who had just been drafted in the first round by the Boston Celtics. His subsequent death from cocaine use marked the beginning of a new drug era, the proliferation of cocaine coupled with its harder-core version—crack.

Drug awareness at that time was largely reactive—not proactive. Schoolchildren—usually in high school—would be shown frightening videos or subjected to lectures about the horrors of drug abuse. I did some research about children and created a program for the bank to underwrite for the community and to be called "Kids Against Drugs." It was more than just a "sponsorship"—the bank was actually putting money behind their words with tangible actions for the good of the community. The primary goal was to help kids in the community understand the dangers of drugs—but secondarily convey to the city that the bank was still a caring part of this community.

The signature event of the "Kids Against Drugs" program was the bank's coordinating with the board of education a series of visits to every classroom in the Central Savannah River Area over the course of several months. This included more than sixty thousand students. Employees of the bank (from branch tellers all the way to top executives) would dress as clowns and literally burst into classrooms unannounced (similar to a fire drill—which research showed made a significant impression on kids). During these visits they would distribute circular "Kids Against Drugs" buttons bearing a small bank logo. The clowns would give the children three easy-to-remember messages about staying away from drugs. A drug hotline number was featured on the back of each button.

The campaign was incredibly successful on every level. The bank got tremendous PR, customers looked at the bank as more than just a place to keep their money, and, most of all, it helped the kids. Calls to the drug hotline tripled over the course of the campaign, with little children turning in pushers in their neighborhoods and seeking help for parents who were users. Fourteen years later, I still point to it as the most significant marketing campaign I ever did.

I desperately wanted the success of this campaign to get out into the mainstream. I knew Augusta was pretty much a small, sleepy market and would not be on the radar of mainstream news groups. That's where my ties to Augusta National entered the picture. George Schultz—a member of the Augusta National and President Ronald Reagan's secretary of state—would host a cocktail reception for local members each time he visited Augusta. My father had received one of these invitations at the time of the "Kids Against Drugs" campaign. My mother was out of town *playing in a golf tournament, so my dad asked if I'd like to go with him. I eagerly accepted, thrilled at the opportunity to meet the Schultzes. I compiled a few of the "Kids Against Drugs" press kits and kept them in the car once we arrived. That night, there were about twenty or so local members gathered for this reception. Mr. Schultz had his guests, which included James Baker, former chief of staff and secretary of the treasury; Nick Brady, secretary of the treasury (also a member); and George Bush, vice president.*

I introduced myself to the wives of these men, figuring they might provide a suitable forum to raise this topic of my little campaign. When Mrs. Baker asked what I did for a living, I casually mentioned the "Kids Against Drugs" campaign. She was impressed and asked for more information. On the way out that night, I left one of the press kits at the front desk with a brief note for Mrs. Baker. A few weeks later the bank chairman received a note from Nancy Reagan congratulating our antidrug efforts. After Mrs. Reagan later came out with her "Just Say No" campaign against drug use, I started to think that maybe I had had something to do with planting that seed, thanks to my Augusta connection.

13 *Gentleman Ben*

OR, "HOW TO FOLLOW THE SUN"

The year was 1967, the year of my favorite Masters Tournament. This was the controversial sixties, crowded with the Vietnam War, hippies, hallucinatory drugs, psychedelic fashions, and demonstrations about every cause imaginable. It was a decade that passed by me like a bullet train. More accurately put, I passed through the sixties like the speeding train, and peering out of that train's window I saw only a blur of these happenings.

Marriage in 1961, first child in 1962, a new house in the mid-sixties, two more children in 1966 and 1968, my husband's new membership at the Augusta National in 1966—all of these goings-on in my personal life gave me little time to keep up with the news and current events. In addition to all of this, I began to attempt to find a golf swing, although my time was limited mostly to family and household duties.

When April 1967 came around, I had only been to one other Masters as the wife of a member. But my excitement about this particular year was increased because my knowledge of the game and its players had grown a great deal. Being surrounded by the Augusta lore and the town's love of the game moved my awareness level light-years ahead from 1966 to the following year of 1967.

Even though the green jacket is the exclusive property of the member and the club, there are some benefits afforded the family of the member, not the least of which is a small, circular green decal with a peel-off adhesive front featuring the logo of the Augusta National. This is part of the identification process at the front gate. I say part because the guard at the gate identifies the occupants of the car, paying far more attention to the people than to the small sticker. In town hardly anyone is lacking in the knowledge of just what that little round circle denotes. As far as the message it carries to the people there, the decal might as well cover most of the windshield.

About a week before the tournament, there was a ceremony we jokingly called the "member's sticker ceremony." In our house, as the children became eligible to drive a car, the ritual took on even more importance, as well as creating a great amount of sibling rivalry. "Who was riding in which car?" "Who was going at what time?" "Her friend went last time?" "It's my turn, her car got the sticker last year?" Etc., etc On and on these girls went with their arguments about riding arrangements for the tournament. It really wasn't about going to see the golf. It was about riding around in the Member's Sticker Car, so all their other friends would be envious.

My three daughters grew up in a house where their getting a member's sticker for their car was a greater thrill than getting a clubhouse badge for the tournament. Not only did they get the celebrity status around tournament time, but once they drove through the main gate, they were allowed to park behind the Bobby Jones Cottage in the members' parking lot and walk directly out on the course by No. 10 tee. All of this was great fun for them, but they had more fun driving around in town with this sticker attached to their windshield because everyone stopped to see just who this person was. There were only a handful of members locally and, therefore, only a few young people with these stickers. This curiosity was not limited to the dues-paying club members: Convenience store employees, car wash attendants, and pedestrians gawked at the sticker, intensely trying to see the small writing at the top and thereby hoping to identify the driver.

Lee:

Within the closed world of Augusta, Georgia, the title "member's daughter" carried with it an element of awe, respect, mystery, wealth, and envy. You were considered part of the privileged few; part of a unique mix of Augusta elite whose circle extended out beyond the city limits and included a powerful blend of names foreign yet familiar to the citizens of my hometown. The physical presence of the club reinforced this image. It rests solidly in the center of town, yet is hidden by thick trees and shrubbery creating an impenetrable wall around the entire club except for a few well-guarded points of entry.

One perk for those in the immediate family of a local member was the prized "member's sticker" for your car. This small, dark green, circular decal featuring the logo of the Augusta National (no words—just the graphic of the United States with a flagstick wedged in the Southeast) had to be displayed on the lower right of the front window of each car in the member's family so the front gate guard could easily view it and wave you through. Rest assured, the sticker alone could not get you past the main gate and onto Magnolia Lane. The member either had to be in the car or at least on the grounds (inside the gate already) and must have notified the guardhouse that visitors would be arriving. Visitors could not exceed three in number, and each member of the family counted as one visitor.

This little sticker created a "class system" among cars—very much mirroring that of the drivers. You could have a beat-up Toyota Corolla with a member's sticker (which I drove in college, by the way) and it would automatically beat

a fully loaded Mercedes without such a sticker. One represented membership—the other money. And everyone knew
money could buy everything but a membership at Augusta
National. I remember trading in my old, worn Toyota when
I graduated from college. The dealer smirked as he circled my
worn little car until his eye caught the member's sticker. "I'll
give you fifteen hundred dollars for the car; two thousand dollars if you leave the Augusta National sticker on."

An amusing "member's sticker" story involved a
boyfriend I dated in my mid-twenties. I was living in
Atlanta and he was working as an eager entry-level stock-
broker. Bob was a good golfer playing to a two or three
handicap and was truly a golf fanatic, particularly when it
came to anything relating to the Augusta National. I'm
sure he dated me through thick and thin with my father's
membership as the golden carrot. He absorbed every detail
of our visits to Augusta, especially my father's stories about
the National. On one of our visits, my father had an extra
member's sticker on the kitchen counter. Bob kept eyeing
the sticker as if it were the Holy Grail—which I'm sure,
within his sphere of importance, it was. Finally, he broke
down and asked if he could please have it for his car. Dad
explained that it was for the immediate family only.
Perhaps this entire episode was constructed as my father's
plot to marry off one of his three daughters.

Gentleman Ben

Lee continues:

*D*uring the Masters Tournament, each member was issued a special set of Masters parking stickers for himself and his immediate family. Dad would get a triangular official sticker, which allowed him to park behind the clubhouse in a reserved parking space featuring his name. Other members of the family would be issued a sticker that featured the word "Member" in bold green letters on a white background. This enabled you to enter through the front gate—usually with several guards stopping six lanes of busy traffic on Washington Road—and slowly cruise down Magnolia Lane toward the bright white clubhouse. At this intersection, another guard would stop any pedestrian traffic to enable you to take a left toward the par-three course and a right to members' parking. This exclusive area, covered in pine straw, included valet parking by state troopers and was adjacent to the tenth tee.

Having "grown up" at the Masters, I never realized the significance of this parking experience. I often wondered as a child why pedestrians would sometimes stop in their tracks and point at our member's sticker in awe as we turned off Magnolia Lane. The amusement for me came later when I began entertaining clients. The experience of actually getting an invitation to the Masters and attending the tournament to watch the golf was often surpassed by the member's sticker experience of cruising down Magnolia Lane. Once a client *asked if we could circle back and "do it again" after we had reached our parking spot. I was often instructed to "slow down" to a noticeable snail's pace so they could take it all in: the lush arc formed by the long rows of old magnolia trees, the crisp white clubhouse centered at the end, the logo of the club formed by bright yellow flowers in the center of the circular front driveway, and the practice areas on each side— usually in full force with the greatest players in the world. It was definitely a unique experience that I only grew to appreciate through the reverence of my guests.*

Robbie:

Having this member's sticker at the 1967 tournament proved a problem for me. This particular year I spent long hours in the stands at the practice area watching Ben Hogan practice. I had long been enthralled with him ever since I had seen the movie of his life, *Follow the Sun*, which I had seen several times in the 1950s. The movie, given bad reviews then and now, was one of my favorites, strange as it might seem with my minimal knowledge of golf at the time. Hogan's unrelenting perseverance and never-ending courage after the car accident in the movie always made me cry. Movies were our only contact with the outside world in that small town in which I grew up. And because television was unheard of and computers a thing of the future, movies controlled our minds and lives to a greater extent than we realized. *Follow the Sun* was not about golf or a golfer, but to me it was a story about a strong man, pure and simple. Glenn Ford, the actor who portrayed Ben Hogan, and Ben Hogan were one and the same to my way of thinking. So in 1967, about fifteen years later, I sat in those stands at the Augusta National and thought how lucky I was to be this close to a living legend from the movies of my childhood.

I sat in those stands at he Augusta National and thought how lucky I was to be this close to a living legend from the movies of my childhood.

Ben Hogan got a standing ovation everywhere he went during the third day of play en route to shooting a 66, which stood up as low round of the day and put him on the periphery of contention for the green jacket following earlier rounds of 74 and 73. It was exciting to be there and feel the appreciation and anticipation of the crowds as he came through the ropes going hole to hole. Gay Brewer was playing well, having somewhat of a point to prove from the previous year, when he had lost in a three-way play-off with Jack Nicklaus and Tommy

Jacobs, then won by Nicklaus. The following and last day of the tournament was shaping up to be a nail-biter. My plans for that final day did not include having much company with me when I went "down Magnolia Lane" because I wanted no distractions or needless conversation while I was following Mr. Hogan from the first tee until the finish.

The next day I got an early start with the household duties and other arrangements for the children so that I could be there for the first shot of Hogan's round, so I could relive the *Follow the Sun* script, much of which was centered around the 1949 auto accident that nearly killed Hogan and his wife Valerie. My husband had already left for the course to take care of his transportation committee duties. I sneaked away from my regular golfing friends and left for the tournament all alone. When I turned onto Washington Road, the traffic was moving slowly and the huge crowds flowed from the public parking lots into the gates like a river making its way to the ocean. As I approached the main gate, the policeman on duty stopped all lanes of traffic to allow me to enter and proceed "down Magnolia Lane." This was a special time, as I drove the car through the arbor of magnolias and headed for the members' parking lot. When I got out of the car, the parking attendant told me my husband wanted to see me in the transportation

126

headquarters. The excited crowd was already gathering around the first tee to be there for Hogan's first shot, as I made my way to see what my husband wanted. When I got to his headquarters, he explained that the wife of one of his best friends needed a ride to the tournament and maybe I could do this favor for him, the favor being that I had to go back to the car, leave the grounds, pick her up, and then return. By then I would have missed the Hogan tee-off, which is exactly what happened.

Ben Hogan had a final-round 77 for a four-day total of 290. Gay Brewer won the Masters that year, but that did not matter to me. I had seen the most exciting player ever play extremely well and give hope to the crowd, hope from an era long ago. It had been 1938 when Ben Hogan received a letter from the National inviting him to play in his first Masters. I was born in 1937. It had taken me a long time to catch up with "the Hawk," but I finally did in April 1967.

Lee:

M y favorite Masters memory is most likely the favorite of many golf fans. It was 1986, the year Jack Nicklaus shot a final-round 65 that included a back-nine 30 to win his sixth green jacket an impressive twenty-three years after he donned his first one.

Gentlemen Only

Many things made this my favorite Masters Tournament of all time. In those years I was just old enough—and just young enough—to believe I was an expert at knowing the best methods and best locales for watching the Masters. After all, I had grown up on the course, and, at age twenty-four, this was my twenty-fourth Masters. I was in my second year of marriage and having a blast. I remember vividly plotting the course and the players to achieve the perfect combination of superb viewing and close proximity to Masters creature comforts: food, beer, rest rooms, and a good crowd.

That Sunday in April 1986 was a spectacular day: The weather was perfect, the flowers were at their peak color, as if on cue, and my husband and I were soaking it all in. One of the most interesting things about being at the Masters versus watching it on television is the theatre-like atmosphere. It's a strange, surreal combination of more than forty thousand people falling quiet to a crucial putt amid the distant thunder of applause and cheering to a well-played ball. A seasoned Masters veteran knows the drill—once you hear the noise, your eyes dart expectantly to the nearest scoreboard to watch the hand-turned number indicating in green (over par) or red (under par) the source of the distant crowd's exultant explosion.

I remember well on this bright Sunday that the action was tight. Many great golfers were in close contention,

Gentleman Ben

producing a diluted gallery spread thin across the entire back nine. We were in a great spot at Amen Corner, a stretch of geography going from eleven green, through the par-three twelfth, and onto the tee and landing area at the thirteenth. From this famous vantage point you can see action encompassing three different holes. When Jack Nicklaus came on the scene at Amen Corner, with son Jackie carrying his bag, the drama of the moment reached an emotional intensity like nothing I had ever been part of before. Something special was unfolding before our eyes. It was more than great golf: It was a tribute to a great man, a legend flexing his muscle nearly a quarter-century after his first triumphant charge at Augusta. It was one of those rare days in life when you find yourself mentally stopping just to inhale and take it all in—the rarity of sheer experiential perfection.

My husband and I decided to follow Nicklaus after he completed Amen Corner. We didn't stop to watch him putt out on thirteen, instead continuing on to number sixteen to take up spectator residence on a spot between the tee and green adjacent to the pond. This is one of my favorite spots to watch the golf. You can see a bit of the action on fifteen green, tee-to-green play on sixteen, and sometimes a few steps away catch a little viewing on six green. There are also several scoreboards in the area as well as nearby food and beverage stands.

When we arrived at sixteen, we easily slid into a front-row spot to watch the players come through. It was here we were able to feel the momentum of Nicklaus's charge that day. It started with a thrilling eagle on fifteen, followed by back-to-back birdies at sixteen and seventeen, with a closing par at eighteen giving him the amazing 30 on the back nine. It was and continues to be one of my favorite sports memories of all time.

My second favorite Masters memory came exactly a year later, in 1987, the year Larry Mize chipped in at eleven for a play-off victory over Greg Norman and Seve Ballesteros.

At the time, I was just starting to get a little "traction" in the early days of my career working as marketing manager for First Union National Bank. I was entertaining a few of the First Union executives at the Masters and still thought of myself as "Miss Know-it-all" when it came to the ultimate Masters viewing experience. My guests were having a ball on that bright final day of the tournament.

When it was evident that a play-off would ensue, I assumed my role as "Course Commander." Masters play-offs start at the tenth hole and continue in a sudden-death format. I told my guests that we should immediately proceed to the eleventh green to get the best viewing spot, even though this would be the second hole of sudden death and there certainly was no guarantee the play-off participants would even make it that far. My guests were immediately up in arms, exclaiming that they would miss the crescendo of the tournament as it concluded back at the tenth. I pressed on and finally convinced them to walk down to eleven, that they would not be disappointed.

As we reached Amen Corner in the area of the eleventh green, it was almost empty. I'm sure my disgruntled guests felt greatly misguided by this silly Augusta female. We waited as Mize and Norman both parred the tenth, while Ballesteros was eliminated with a bogey. It was on to eleven for Mize and the Shark. Suddenly, my male guests were a little more hushed in their condemnations of my viewing strategy. In the end, we had the ultimate front-row position as Mize, an Augusta native no less, chipped in from almost fifty yards away for the victory. The crowd exploded, once again providing a great signature sports moment at the Masters for both me and my (very impressed) guests. After that day, the whole story circulated around the bank, and my career was given a gentle boost within the boys' club.

Arnold Palmer, at the Masters.

14 Gentleman Living Legend

Or, "Dinner with a special couple"

In the early part of the 1800s, banking in Augusta, as elsewhere in Georgia, was on loose footing. Sound business development and stability in established businesses were crippled by the risky financial policies of the banking industry. The organization of the Georgia Railroad in 1833, to some extent, corrected the faulty banking business practices that existed before the formation of the Georgia Railroad and Banking Company in 1835.

The Georgia Railroad and Banking Company became more than a bank in Augusta, as the town grew in size and commerce developed rapidly in the area. The bank took it upon itself to help with political and social activities as well as the ordinary monetary business that banks normally handle. Augustans grew to expect the strong arm of this bank's influence to reach into every community project and even some personal situations that the general public did not realize. The founding fathers of the proposed Augusta National found out about this power firsthand as they began to obtain the property on Washington Road that would later be their golf course. Everyone who has read anything about the early years when Roberts, Jones, and their local influential contingency tried to get possession of the land, knows about the problems that existed with the Fruitland Nurseries and the sought-after acres. Enter the Georgia Railroad Bank. They held a first mortgage on a debt of sixty thousand dollars incurred by the owners of the property.

In the early 1960s, when I was getting acquainted with the town, I heard numerous rumors or truths about the controversy that went on between the group trying to obtain the powerful Georgia Railroad Bank and the Washington Road property. Mr. Roberts is said to have become a little less than enamored with those banking powers at one point. So much so that he carried on business with a much smaller bank, a competitor to the Georgia Railroad and Banking Company. He not only carried on business at that time with the smaller bank, but he never forgot the favors they did for him while he was desperately trying to get his project off the ground. The evidence of his fierce appreciation was shown later when the invitation to membership was extended to the president of this smaller bank, and the president of the larger bank was ignored. One of Mr. Roberts's most redeeming character traits was that he never forgot any favor or assistance someone extended him. On the other hand, he remembered the bad for as long as he remembered the good. Therefore, the powers at the top of the Georgia Railroad and Banking Company were in for a lifetime of being on Mr. Roberts's bad side. Long after his enemies there were gone or no longer in power, Roberts punished the descendants for the sins of their predecessors. After the Augusta National became the most prestigious club anywhere, the smaller bank was able to keep the club's business and had its top employee invited to membership in the National.

When I came to the city, the Georgia Railroad Bank was on the corner of Seventh and Broad Streets. It was a rather imposing building for the downtown area at that time, making sure that citizens knew about its power. The bank also owned several adjacent buildings in that block of Broad Street, including the small and rather time-worn building next door to its large and well-kept facade. This building housed the Town Tavern Restaurant, a business owned and operated by my husband and his family. Looking back, I can see that being close to power always made my husband feel better.

The Town Tavern was first opened by my husband's father in 1937, a time before there were any other well-established restaurants or franchised food businesses in the area. The Tavern's reputation was built on entrees like their prime beef, live Maine lobsters, she-crab soup, and homemade dressings. My father-in-law took great pride in his business, but my husband always reminded him of the note he had signed for his father to open up the business in the first place. However, this didn't really bother my father-in-law, "Mr. Willie," as he was affectionately called by almost everyone in the town. His restaurant was his life. His customers were his joy. His favorite thing to do was slip into a booth with a friend having lunch and discuss *Dante's Inferno*, drawing from his voracious appetite for reading. He

His favorite thing to do was slip into a booth with a friend having lunch and discuss Dante's Inferno, drawing from his voracious appetite for reading.

was self-educated and loved to talk with other people about any and all sorts of things. His love for his business, the lack of competition, and World War II turned the business into a thriving restaurant that remained that way for many years.

The Masters Tournament and the Town Tavern became business partners of sorts, due in part to their sharing the same town in the month of April. The crowds that came for the tournament would hear about the wonderful steaks, prime beef carefully selected by Mr. Willie, the live Maine lobsters flown in fresh that very day, and the friendly atmosphere of the restaurant created by the family who owned the business. Long lines formed during the tournament, and individuals were given a number to keep order. Local people knew to stay away during tournament time, unless their curiosity got the best of them and they ventured to the Tavern to catch a glimpse of some celebrity who might just be dining there. "Is that Bing Crosby in that dark booth across the way?" "Is that man standing in the bar the player who is leading the tournament?"

My husband played not just golf, but also tennis, badminton, bridge, and all other card games. His father, Mr. Willie, never played golf. In his words, he "never played anything." He just loved to work at that restaurant. The only time I ever saw him get truly upset was when the word "Atlanta" was mentioned. "That town was just an inland hub for a railroad. It doesn't have the big Savannah River for commerce and trade or any of the culture, history, or fame that Augusta enjoyed long before those northern folks took over Atlanta and made it into the successful big city it became. It really should not have become the metropolis it became," was Mr. Willie's complete theory about Atlanta, and he would give this lecture almost daily. I sometimes had to turn my head away to hide the smile on my face because I knew that those same

Clifford Roberts and Mr. Willie were very similar in some ways. They both had tunnel vision about their projects— the Augusta National for Roberts and the Town Tavern for Mr. Willie.

northern folks were at least somewhat responsible for some of the successes in his hometown as well. Clifford Roberts and Mr. Willie were very similar in some ways. They both had tunnel vision about their projects—the Augusta National for Roberts and the Town Tavern for Mr. Willie. However, the only time they shared the stage was in April when patrons, writers, and celebrities came for the Cliff Roberts tournament and dined at Mr. Willie's restaurant. I do not think they knew each other, but they shared some of the ideas and ideals that would have made them good friends had they met.

Progress forced the Georgia Railroad Bank to think about building an enormous, multistoried new building to house their bank, offices for lease, and a dining club. The plan was to tear down the old bank and rebuild that modern skyscraper on the same site. The Town Tavern was told they would have to move because the bank would need the additional land for the new building. These were difficult times for Mr. Willie. He was much older now, and change of any kind made him nervous. But, having no choice, the new restaurant was built on Seventh Street near the levee. Larger dining areas, more parking facilities, and modern kitchens would have been the dream of any other restaurant owner, but not Mr. Willie. He and I longed for the same thing, the old Tavern housed in the rather shabby building on Broad Street. After all, how does one incorporate in a new building the echoes of sounds from the past, smells from all that delicious food as it was cooked, and the ghosts of people no longer living? He and I were part of a large number of people who never liked the new restaurant as much as the old one.

~

Lee:

*O*ne year I became interested in learning about wine. I knew something about typical California chardonnay and was eager to learn about French wines. I scoured bookstores, buying up volumes of guides, history books, reviews, etc. As anyone who has attempted self-teaching when it comes to French wines knows, it can be quite intimidating. Reading the labels alone can be a complicated task.

One day I mentioned my new interest in wine to my father while visiting him in Augusta. We were planning to have lunch at the National (or, as my father said, "at the morgue," since there usually were no more than five members on the grounds at Augusta at any given time.) He casually mentioned that I should see the wine cellar at the National. I didn't even know a cellar existed. You always knew the National was created for and about golf. There were no tennis courts, no swimming pools, you couldn't hold your daughter's wedding reception here—this place was strictly golf. So when I heard about the wine cellar, I was a bit surprised.

After we were seated at our tables and sipping our beers, Dad summoned Frank Carpenter over to the table. He was a large African-American man who somewhat resembled a gentler, kinder version of Don King. He was the major caretaker of the wine cellar. Dad asked Frank to give me the nickel tour of the wine cellar.

We exited through a door in the Trophy Room and followed a narrow hallway to the cellar's entrance. As the door opened, I was blown away by the impressive order and unbelievable selection of wines. It started with French reds, everything from the most sought-after Romanée-Conti to the decadent Château Pétrus, then French whites including my favorites—Montrachet and Puligny-Montrachet—continuing onto domestic reds, whites, and other regions. It was such a great experience to see all of these wines I had been reading about for months and to hear pearls of wisdom from Frank Carpenter about selected bottles and vintages. It was one of my favorite—and unexpected—Augusta National memories.

Robbie:

As strange as it may sound, the newly built bank did provide a place for me to have one of my favorite dinners of all times. The Pinnacle Club was the name given the Georgia Railroad Bank's top floors in their recently constructed building. The invitation to this particular dinner came from an acquaintance of my husband, an old friend who also was a member at the Augusta National. Over the years this other member had become close friends with a golf legend from Texas, a place that seemed to grow those kinds of folks. When he invited us to dinner as his guest, he neglected to tell me who this celebrity was, only stating something like, "You and your husband will have a great deal in common with him and his wife, so the dinner should be most enjoyable for everyone."

We were to meet them in the ornately decorated lobby of the Pinnacle Club at seven o'clock. My curiosity about the identity of the guests was temporarily forgotten as we entered the elaborate new bank, took the high-tech elevators to the top floor, and stepped onto the Oriental rug covering the lobby's hallway. Oil paintings, expensive furnishings, and huge chandeliers gave these surroundings an elegance I had not seen in any other new building in Augusta. However, this only temporarily distracted me because standing there before me, holding out his hand to introduce himself, was the legend, the one I had read and heard so much about. He then introduced his wife, who was many years younger than he. Immediately, I understood what our host had meant about our having a great deal in common.

We made our way to the dining room and were seated at the best table in the room with a perfect view of the big Savannah River outside the large windows to our right. We ordered the food, which was served with promptness and style, and the dinner conversation went on as if we had all known each other many years. At one point in the conversation, the legend said that he had met his wife at a tournament, and that they loved to play golf together. He further stated that on their next visit he and his wife would like to have a match with my husband and me. This never happened, but that's all right, because when you have been in the presence of a legend like Byron Nelson, even for just a few hours, the greatness of the man lasts from that time forward.

⌒

Lee:

*B*ack in the early nineties I traveled quite a bit because of my job. On one of my long trips from L.A. to New York, I sat next to a distinguished-looking man in his fifties. We engaged in small talk that led to deeper discussion. The story of my dad's membership at the Augusta National eventually worked its way into the conversation, and that sparked the usual inquiry of insider information. I genuinely liked this guy—he was warm, funny, and enjoyable to talk with. He was a trader with an old, established Wall Street firm and controlled the stocks of several household brands. He also was an avid golfer who had played almost every famous course in the world—except Augusta. I, on the other hand, am a huge fan of Wall Street and have long been fascinated by the energy of the market. By the end of our flight, I had proposed an exchange: I would arrange a round of golf at Augusta for him if he would provide me and my mom "a day in his life" on the floor of the New York Stock Exchange. We exchanged business cards with a promise to reconnect.

I called Dad and got some available golf dates. The Wall Street trader brought two CEOs—the head of a large telecommunications company and the head of a major airline. They flew down to Augusta on a private jet, were entertained by Dad, and bestowed upon him the ever-appropriate case of scotch at the conclusion of the day. My dad genuinely liked this Wall Street trader and his guests and asked about them frequently over the years. My mom and I had our thrilling tour of the New York Stock Exchange as the guest of this gentleman—it was a day I'll never forget. This was one of many "memory barters" that transpired over my years as the daughter of a member at Augusta.

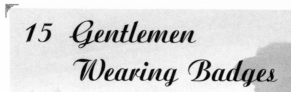

15 Gentlemen Wearing Badges

OR, "ARE YOU A PLAYER'S WIFE?"

In today's world, getting a series badge for the Masters Tournament is like winning the Irish Sweepstakes in the sports world. The numerous questions about how to obtain membership in the prestigious club have been replaced by just trying to get in to see the event once in a lifetime. Begging, borrowing, and stealing are all possibilities when it comes to getting there for a day or just an hour. Even the practice rounds that precede the regulation four days of tournament play are now sought after as aggressively as the series badges were in the past. As in the old golf saying—"Every stroke makes someone happy"—every twist and turn in the format of the Masters makes someone happy and someone sad. Recently, I heard someone in a small town lament that they at one time got to use a friend's tickets on certain days, but now that scalping of tickets is legal in Georgia, these folks are no longer offered the use of those tickets. Tickets are sold for a big price now. From the "other side," whether heaven or hell, Mr. Roberts must be screaming and yelling in protest of this practice.

Gentlemen Wearing Badges

In the mid-sixties, when I first starting going to the tournament, practice-round tickets were readily available and series badges were not too difficult to find. All of this changed when Mr. Roberts decided there were too many people and too little space during the practice rounds for the spectators to see the tournament adequately. So he decided to limit the number of tickets to the practice rounds and cut the number of series badges allotted each patron. That is to say, if you were originally receiving four badges, under his new rule you would now receive only two under his new rule. In addition to this came the news that the practice-round tickets would be sold separately. In a never-ending battle to police the tournament for the purpose of improvement, Mr. Roberts never worried about the hardship these rules would work on his patrons. His only concern had been and would always be the quality of the tournament.

In addition to the practice-round ticket and the patron's series badge, there is the coveted Trophy Room badge of which a certain number can be purchased—purchased only through a member and with the approval of the "committee." Wearing this badge will grant the owner the right to pass through the ropes surrounding the heavily guarded clubhouse facility and into the Trophy Room. There the badge wearer can buy food and drink, use the private rest rooms, and, most importantly, see and be

The Trophy Room provided a dining experience that was just another part of the Paradise we knew as the Augusta National.

seen. The Trophy Room and the umbrella area just out-side are lodging places for some people who come to the tournament—meaning they never leave there to see any part of the golf except what is televised on the many TV sets placed for viewing in this area.

I was walking through this area one day after having been to that closet-sized bathroom Mr. Roberts provided for us women, when I was hailed over to a table of "Trophy Room Lodgers," all locals who had purchased those sought-after badges. They were eager to have me stand there and converse or even join them so that other people in the area could see them talking to someone with a "Clubhouse" badge, thereby impressing the surrounding groups. Moving away as quickly as I could politely do so, I remarked that I was eager to get down to number fifteen to see the action going on there. There were gasps in unison from the people seated at the table: "You mean you are going down there with all those people, when you could just stay here and watch it on television?" As I was leaving through the ropes to go back to the golf course, I glanced back to see the group at the table shaking their heads in disbelief.

The *piece de resistance* is the Clubhouse Badge, reserved only for members and their immediate family, certain dignitaries, players, and their families. This badge allows the holder to pass through all gates, doors, the pro shop, and the main clubhouse, everywhere except up that staircase with the shiny brass "Gentlemen Only" sign.

There have been some exceptions to the qualification procedure in the past. Not being allowed in certain areas just did not sit well with this particular gentleman I will call "Big John," who was not a member of the club but would have sacrificed his firstborn son for the chance to become a member.

For many years Big John lived in Augusta, wheeling and dealing and accumulating some wealth as well as a reputation for spending and buying whatever he wanted. Every year he seemed to come up with a Clubhouse Badge for himself and some of his family members, as if he were a member in good standing of the club. Everyone in the town was aware that overtures were constantly being made to somehow get him an invitation for membership, but no progress could be made. This lack of interest in him as a member of the National did not deter him from entertaining other guests there constantly. Of course, he had to comply with all the necessary rules of the National in order to entertain there because he was a guest and his guests were guests of the host of whom he himself was a guest. His moving to Atlanta a few years later provided him even more opportunities to bring friends and business associates from there to the National. He called on all of the old friends who were local members of the National to help him with his constant flow of guests from Atlanta. Of course, they did not mind doing this because he was extremely generous with his thank-you gifts. It is considered taboo to have any commercial compensation in exchange for entertaining guests, but a rather nice gift of some unique nature is acceptable. His gifts were carefully chosen and well appreciated so that the next time he called with another guest, the answer was an automatic "OK."

Because of all this entertaining and politicking on the grounds of the club, Big John came to know rather well one of the high-level administrative assistants in the front office of the club. The woman loved to spend time in

Gentlemen Wearing Badges

Atlanta, enjoying the shopping opportunities and Fox Theater shows. So the two of them were able to make an exchange of assets that made both of them quite happy. She would get him some Clubhouse Badges for the Masters, and he would let her use his downtown condominium for her Atlanta trips. As far as I know, there were no questions asked by the big guys running the tournament. But my theory was that ignoring this arrangement was easier than having him elected to membership. After all, what's one week out of the year compared to a lifetime?

And then there were the badgeless people who came every year to the Augusta area with no tickets, badges, or even any hopes of getting any. Why did they come? It was several years before I realized that there were hordes of people coming to the area, staying in motels for the entire tournament time, and never going anywhere near the gates of the Augusta National. The closest they ever got to the National was the many souvenir stands out on Washington Road, which gave them the opportunity to buy merchandise that was not authorized by the Augusta National. Shirts, caps, banners, and all sorts of souvenir items printed with the word "Augusta"—not Augusta National, "Golf capital of the world"—but no patented logo like the green map with the flag stuck in the Georgia area—items like this could be bought rather cheaply at these stands.

So here is what was happening with the badgeless people. They would leave their homes in the North with three feet of snow still on the ground, head south to Augusta, stay anywhere close by, play golf at all the public courses around the area, send postcards to their friends back home with their snow, and, of course, buy lots of souvenirs to take back home with them on Sunday after completion of the Masters. The only Masters they had seen had been on their television screens in their motel rooms, but the folks back home would never know that they had not been to the Masters, because they had all those gifts from Augusta to give away upon arriving back at their frozen neighborhoods. Then there was all the conversation about the flowers, crowds, sights, and sounds of the South, etc., etc., while the friends

Then there was all the conversation about the flowers, crowds, sights, and sounds of the South, etc., etc., while the friends and neighbors turned green with envy.

and neighbors turned green with envy. The badgeless had a nice trip, played golf, and got to impress their friends when they returned home. Who cares if they had no ticket or badge to the tournament? It really did not matter to them. They had a great time anyway.

Gentlemen Wearing Badges

Then there was the local badge-less group. They had a more difficult problem when it came to not having tickets or badges, especially when friends or relatives called from another town to ask for a place to stay and possibly a ticket to the tournament. They could provide the place to stay, but telling anyone that they could not get tickets would be just a little embarrassing. So to solve the problem, many upper-middle-class people in the town would put their $300,000 houses on the rental market for the week of the tournament, and they would take off for Sea Island or Hilton Head for the week. Problem solved. It gave them an out, as far as the ticket situation was concerned, and the "little woman of the house" got a little extra grocery money upon returning from the beach. Who wanted to stay here anyway with all those parties going on, the traffic jams, and outsiders crowding the restaurants and golf courses?

Many upper-middle-class people in the town would put their $300,000 houses in the rental market for the week of the tournament, and they would take off for Sea Island or Hilton Head for the week. Problem solved.

Badges! Badges! Badges! All different kinds everywhere! It is not uncommon to see a woman wearing a big hat or carrying a pocketbook adorned with badges she has collected over the years at every tournament. But the

153

badge that represents the current year must be displayed in a prominent place so that security can check the patron's eligibility with just a glance. Some badges are nontransferable. In addition to the members' and Trophy Room badges, there are officials' and workers' badges. The most frequently asked question by the average spectator of those of us with member's badges was, "Are you a player's wife?" On most occasions, there were more players and their wives on the course than there were members and their wives. Mr. Roberts came up with this great plan to keep everyone labeled and in the proper place at all times—that is, except for "Big John."

～

Lee:

*T*he highlight of my teen golfing years was the Masters Tournament. The excitement was not so much the tournament itself, but the days leading up to the opening round. That was when I worked on my father's transportation committee.*

Each Augusta National member is assigned an area of responsibility during the tournament, and it is his duty to fully execute all tasks involved in that area in accordance with the strict standards dictated by Mr. Roberts. My father's chairmanship of the transportation committee included securing the vehicles to be used during the tournament by the players, the press, and other officials. Of course, the bulk of the work was delegated to a small group of local businessmen eager to serve on an "official" committee and obtain the cherished admission to the Masters Tournament.

A small and rather exclusive group of teenagers were hired to pick up these Cadillacs from dealerships, drive them to an empty lot inside the gates of the National, and place all the appropriate official vehicle credentials with the car. One of the perks was being able to drive a golf cart around the grounds during the practice rounds and behind the scenes during the tournament. Unfortunately, at that time females were forbidden to do this—we could not even be transported as passengers. So the irony was that even though my father chaired the committee on which my peers served, I was prohibited from doing my job as quickly as they could. I had to walk everywhere. That's why I was usually assigned the office-related task of checking in the players and press officials. After checking in each one, I would hand the keys over to one of my male coworkers, who would get to drive the player (Arnie included) to his official car in the cherished golf cart. This rule was amended sometime after Mr. Roberts passed on, but too late for me to have benefited. Believe it or not, I find this change of also letting girls drive the carts somewhat unfortunate. Sometimes it's more appropriate to embrace tradition and work within its framework, rather than trying to break tradition and destroy all things around it.

Gentlemen Only

Years later, when I started entertaining clients during the Masters, I heard them repeatedly remark about how cheap the food and beverages were: Sandwiches for a dollar and beers (poured from the bottle back then) for a buck fifty, and the quality was amazing. The sandwiches were always fresh, the beer ice cold.

Growing up at the Masters, I pretty much sampled all of the tournament sandwiches and arrived at my favorite at an early age: the egg salad on white. Something about the freshness of the salad on soft white bread is a symphony to the taste buds. When I would entertain guests, they would all watch in disbelief as I consumed two or three of these great little sandwiches over the course of the day. My guests would select the usual—ham and rye, club, or barbeque (my second favorite) until I coerced them to sample an egg salad. After that the addiction begins.

I still have friends from years back who say the egg salad sandwich at the Masters is one of their favorite foods of all time. Now that I'm a "grown-up" and considered to be quite the New York "foodie"—always in the know about the latest, hottest restaurants and wine lists—the Masters 'egg salad still makes my top-ten list of favorite foods.

16 A Gentlewoman's Short Takes

Or, "Corn bread, Wandering Jew, and Sunsets"

Years later I am a long way from all those grand lifestyles, famous people, and golf played on special courses, far away in more ways than can be measured in miles. Hardly anything is the same now as it was in my "other life" in Augusta. But there are occasions when those flashbacks come out of nowhere to remind me that there is "common ground" or a connection between the past and present.

Corn Bread

Almost every time I lift the heavy cast-iron skillet from the stove drawer to make my favorite recipe for old Southern corn bread, I remember the first time I discovered that "down Magnolia Lane" they served corn bread with every meal. Their fascination with corn bread shocked me because where I come from it's a survival food, not a luxury. We in the South usually serve corn bread with the appropriate accompanying food— like turnip greens and corn bread—not caviar and corn bread. To each his own.

158

A Gentlewoman's Short Takes

Firewood

When I build a fire in my wood stove, my mind invariably goes back to the giant fireplaces in the Augusta National's main clubhouse and the perfect fires already burning in them when members and guests arrived. My fires here burn well also, but the bark is still on the logs when they are placed in the stove, not clean-shaven like those at the end of Magnolia Lane. But when the fire gets really going or, as the Europeans say, "When the fire is marching," logs of any kind will do. And there is a special warmth given off by those logs that come from your own property and cut with your own hands. There might be some members at the end of Magnolia Lane who have never felt this kind of warmth.

Wandering Jew vs. Red Geraniums

Webster's Dictionary defines wandering jew as: any of three trailing plants, *tradescantia albiflora*, *T. fluminensis* or *Zembrina pendula*, native to tropical America, usually having variegated foliage and widely grown as house plants. I define it as a "dull" plant partly because during my formative years, every poor person in South Georgia had some wandering jew, if they had nothing else in the way of plants or shrubbery. However, this is not why I dislike the plant. It is also dull in color, greenish or purplish, and dull in form, falling loosely in all directions.

Every year just before the Masters Tournament, the club was given an extra amount of sprucing up and "window dressing." New hanging baskets were placed all around the porches of the main clubhouse and anywhere else a basket could be hung. About a week before a certain upcoming Masters, my husband and I were headed "down Magnolia Lane" when I spotted the gigantic hanging baskets all around the buildings—not just any hanging baskets, but baskets loaded with huge wandering jew plants. The scream that came from my throat startled my husband so badly that he stopped the car abruptly and asked, "What in the hell is the matter with you???" "It's that wandering jew!!!!" Then I further explained that with all those white buildings, red geraniums would look much better than that dull, dark vine trailing down in all directions. Being the "Mr. Take Charge" that he was, especially if he thought well of the proposal, he immediately called the manager and gave him my message. By late that same afternoon, the wandering jew baskets were removed and replaced with bright red geranium baskets. This has been the tradition ever since.

Gift Giving

Christmas and birthdays generate memories about the best of times for most people and the special gifts received at those times. For me some of the best gifts I ever received came from Clifford Roberts. When he was alive, he spent a great deal of time, effort, and money purchasing just the right gifts for those people who had worked on the previous tournament. This included the members who, during the tournament, were referred to as Officials. Some years the wives of these officials and workers were given a different gift than the men. Among my favorite presents were a beautiful silk scarf with the logo of the National in the corners, a gold pin in the shape of the logo, and many other beautiful and unusual things. But my very favorite gift was a sterling wine trivet engraved by the the Crown Jewelers in London. This trivet featured the clubhouse surrounded by the flower that represents each of the eighteen holes. The man had excellent taste in gifts, and he knew how to show appreciation better than anyone.

Sunsets

It was a picture-perfect November day, that kind we have on rare occasions here in the South—the kind of day that makes you glad you live in the South and makes you temporarily forget about all those gnats, flies, and mosquitoes. The sweltering heat and drowning humidity of summer had gone and the reward of the cool November days made life good again. Sunsets get better in the fall in the South.

I recently sat on a rough crosstie that lines the rose garden, watching the November sun sink behind brilliant clouds. There was nothing hindering my view because we grow cut flowers here and trees are not wanted. I remembered another sunset in another place: We were seated in those cool metal chairs out under the big oak behind the main clubhouse on one of those perfect November afternoons, just before the sun sank from view. There was nobody else around that afternoon at the beautiful Augusta National except for us and our guests. We sat there mesmerized by the place and the show the sun was providing. A lone member left the pro shop and came slowly up the hill headed for his cottage for the night. When he saw us and looked out across the acres of green toward the sinking sun, he remarked as he continued to walk, "Another day in paradise, huh?"

An outdoor seating area at Augusta National, with the Eisenhower
Cottage in the background, providing a panoramic view of the course
and a great place to watch sunsets in the western sky.